OXFORD BOOK OF

Sonnets

THE
OXFORD BOOK OF
Sonnets

EDITED BY
JOHN FULLER

OXFORD
UNIVERSITY PRESS

OXFORD
UNIVERSITY PRESS

Great Clarendon Street, Oxford OX2 6DP

Oxford University Press is a department of the University of Oxford.
It furthers the University's objective of excellence in research, scholarship,
and education by publishing worldwide in

Oxford New York

Auckland Bangkok Buenos Aires Cape Town Chennai
Dar es Salaam Delhi Hong Kong Istanbul Karachi Kolkata
Kuala Lumpur Madrid Melbourne Mexico City Mumbai Nairobi
São Paulo Shanghai Singapore Taipei Tokyo Toronto

Oxford is a registered trade mark of Oxford University Press
in the UK and in certain other countries

Published in the United States
by Oxford University Press Inc., New York

British Library Cataloguing in Publication Data

Data available

Library of Congress Cataloging in Publication Data

The Oxford book of sonnets / edited by John Fuller.
Includes bibliographical references and index.
1. Sonnets, English. 2. Sonnets, American. I. Fuller, John
PR1195.S5O94 2000 823'.04208—dc21 00–036757

ISBN 0–19–280389–1

1 3 5 7 9 10 8 6 4 2

Printed in Spain by
Book Print S.L., Barcelona

CONTENTS

CONTENTS

CONTENTS

CONTENTS

ix

CONTENTS

CONTENTS

CONTENTS

CONTENTS

CONTENTS

CONTENTS

CONTENTS

CONTENTS

CONTENTS

CONTENTS

CONTENTS

CONTENTS

INTRODUCTION

1

THE arrangement of the sonnets in this anthology is by chrono-
logical order of poets, according to the year of their birth. An
arrangement by subject would have ultimately proved too crude
a net to trawl with, since a large number of sonnets would have
eluded thematic boundaries, however finely defined. The present
arrangement has the simple virtue of making historical develop-
ment perfectly plain to the attentive reader.

The history of poetry in English cannot, however, be repre-
sented by the history of a particular form, not even of this, the
best known and most versatile of the free-standing verse-
forms, alive and well after over 450 years of life in English.
Chaucer wrote no sonnets. Nor did Dryden or Pope. There are
poets of the first rank who are not best, or barely at all, repre-
sented by their few sonnets: Byron, Blake, and Browning come
to mind. In the history of the sonnet, Charles Tennyson Turner
figures more largely than his brother Alfred, Merrill Moore will
loom in place of Marianne, and Hartley Coleridge may even
claim as much space as his father (though here I have not
allowed it). There are poets who should have been sonneteers
but were not (the Brontës, Wallace Stevens). There are whole
traditions to which the sonnet has no access (Whitman/
Sandburg/Williams or Lawrence/Hughes) and there are figure-
heads in our own era (Eliot, Pound) who were bad at sonnets

for various reasons. Pound is an interesting case, for simply not seeing the point:

> The well-groomed sonnet is to truth preferred;
> Let us be all things so we're not absurd,
> Dabble with forms and damn the verity.

He was no doubt following his admired Landor ('A better use of time I know | Than tossing shuttles to an fro') with the added benefit of exasperation with the antique exclamatory style of popular late-Victorian sonneteers like Lang or Lee-Hamilton. But Pound missed a chance here, for he might have found models for his satiric side in a poet such as Meredith, and it is in grotesque or incongruous observation that the sonnet renews itself in Pound's time: Hardy, Robinson, Frost, Sassoon, Ransom, and the rest. It is this tradition, after all, which inaugurated the third great era of the sonnet in English that reached a peak in Auden (the first two were the half-centuries between Sidney and Habington, and between Charlotte Smith and Elizabeth Barrett Browning).

And yet, despite these implicit lacunae in our history, the sonnet proposes 'verities' of its own which do have a representative status. When the sonnet arrived in the Tudor Court about three centuries after its invention it was already freighted with the Petrarchan idealism which the Elizabethans went on to celebrate and ironize. Idealism provides a natural entrée into the brilliant metaphysical or religious philosophizing that dignifies the early seventeenth-century sonnet in Chapman, Shakespeare, Donne, or Habington; while the kind of private experience of the public world which turns up freshly in Milton not only reflects the obvious political concerns of the mid-seventeenth century, but casts an attenuated shadow over the very few sonnets written over the ensuing hundred years.

It is something of a surprise in this sonnet-desert to come across the knowing erotic rakishness of Cotton's delineation of his four rural sisters, but the attitudes are no more uncharacteristic or 'objectionable' than Barnes's desire in the previous century to pass the lips of his lady as wine in order to pass in due course close to her genitals as urine. The sonnet had become perfectly capable of expressing and concentrating the male whims of each age. The women who revived the sonnet in the 1780s (Charlotte Smith, Helen Williams, Anna Seward, and others) were understandably notable Miltonists, as was Coleridge in his polemical sonnets and Wordsworth in his whole conduct of the form. For Wordsworth, Milton's technical developments towards organic unity in the sonnet were quite as important as his sense of the possible occasions of a form that is not in a trivial sense occasional at all.

The Romantic period simply saw a vast extension of the range of the sonnet from, say, that of Tasso who had divided his sonnets into Love Sonnets, Heroical Sonnets, and Sacred and Moral Sonnets. It had long been used for dedications and eulogies as well as for its primary function in erotic or religious devotion, but it is not until the Romantics that the full development of the domestic, the visionary, and the nature sonnet occurs. The impulse linking these kinds of sonnet is one acutely observed by Coleridge: 'in which some lonely feeling is developed'. The sonnet, above all other lyric forms, with its unique combination of emotional intensity and argued development, gives the reader a powerful sense not only of a mind in communion with itself, but a mind in which thought significantly proceeds to a point of greater understanding.

Some aspects of the sonnet in this period have been neglected by anthologists (the key role of women writers, for example, or the vibrancy of the comic and satiric sonnet) and I hope to have somewhat remedied this neglect (for example, Hood's 'cold transparent ham' is more authentic than his Keatsian imitations). However, it has at least been generally acknowledged that the earlier nineteenth century was a more fruitful breeding-ground for sonnets than the later. Even the hostile Landor succumbed after his fashion. In his tribute to Arthur Walker the clusters of rhyme and assonance and the embracing rhyme at beginning and end (*abcd*[*e*]*b*[*e*]*bfg*[*h*][*h*]*ia*) are about as far as I go in this anthology in admitting eccentricity of rhyme-scheme, but the effect is comparable to some of the conscious experiments of Coleridge and Keats (who wanted 'sandals more interwoven and complete to fit the naked foot of Poesy' than traditional rhyme-schemes allowed). This small example of fascination and dislike represents, incidentally, a more widespread attraction to, and distrust of, the form. In our day, many American poets have conscientiously adopted the verdict of Pound quoted above, while instinctively, or even with apparent secrecy, resorting to the writing of sonnets over-reliant on revived Renaissance tropes. Aiken's 'And in the Human Heart' is an interesting example of such a policy, well dabbled and yet soggy with verities. Eberhart and Berryman both hoarded their immature sequences, to no significant effect. Robert Lowell might have been the Milton of our time but in his anxiety to avoid 'the themes and gigantism of the sonnet' ended up in *History* free-associating like Pound's *Cantos*, and so produced neither one thing nor the other. It is something to do not only with his developed resistance to the rhetorical patterning of the pentameter, but also to a cavalier attitude to the idea of the sequence, both formal requirements fully accepted by a poet like Auden (for example), who well knew the value of resisting resistance to the established character of verse-forms.

In the second half of the nineteenth century, apart from the eccentric genius of Hopkins, the most successful vein of sonneteering is utterly luminous, direct, and simple. And once again it is women poets who seem to be best at it, notably Christina Rossetti, but also lesser and neglected poets such as 'Michael Field' or Alice Meynell. Much of the rest of this period seems to be marking time, finding nothing new that had not essentially been performed by Wordsworth or Keats.

All poets in their sonnets have their weaknesses, even Wordsworth with his dutiful tourist occasions, his double negatives, and debased machinery of 'frolic Loves' or Keats with his self-dramatizing. Any habitual sonneteer will in the end expose himself, as Tennyson Turner does with his ready sententiousness about trivial incidents or Clare with his reliance on simply listing in delight the things that he had seen. Or the extraordinary case of Merrill Moore, who believed that sonnets 'require excitement in at least one line' and constructed over 50,000 of them, many dependent on that slenderest of excuses. But whatever the poetic status of the author, a good poem always emerges from a successful negotiation with form, and in all these cases it has long been an unarguable truth that the sonnet has been able to bring out the best in them, at their different levels of best. Tennyson Turner, for example, does have a reliable instinct for the ways in which the sonnet relates the particular and the general (165[1]: 'In the great

---

[1] These numbers refer to the numbered sonnets in the anthology.

voice of Roman history | I lost the pleading of the window-bee') and can provide enlarging frissons quite as well as Keats (163, where Letty's epiphanic but Aryan 'golden hair' seems at once to bless and defy the frontier-conscious Europe of the early nineteenth century).

2

The sonnet is a dualistic structure, formalizing the essence of drama in statement and response. In its origins in thirteenth-century Sicily, the sestet of the Italian sonnet may have had a different and answering music to that of the octave (typically *abbaabba cdecde* or *cdcdcd*). Certainly its defiance of the expectation of a second stanza complementary in length to the first is crucial to the satisfying imbalance of structure (8 : 6). The English sonnet, in quatrains and couplets (*ababcdcdefefgg*), more obviously goes in a different direction, which shares the confined structure of logic (4 : 4 : 4 : 2). Other English variants with similarly balanced components (between twelve and eighteen lines in some Elizabethan sequences, sixteen in the admired 'Modern Love' of Meredith) are further from the essence of the sonnet than are the dwarfs and monsters that preserve such a proportion of imbalance, Hopkins's curtal sonnets (6 : 4½), for example, or the third sonnet of Auden's 'The Quest' (12 : 9). The beauty of the Italian form has been ascribed to its similarities to Platonic or Pythagorean musical ratios that were also incorporated into classical architecture, and it is frequently described as a natural organic structure, like an acorn in its cup or, in William Bell Scott's view, the advance and retreat of the tide. The critic is concerned with the achieved effect of the form's history and practice, says Scott,

Not the steps, but what remains;

See the analogue, ebb and flow, —
Beautiful, yes, look at it near, —
The flow, the ebb returning so, —
It is at last art's perfect sphere.

His contrast with the English sonnet is not disrespectful, but raises the crucial structural issue:

But not the less our Shakespeare knew
Another way; by full discourse
To show his picture as it grew,
Worked out in many-sided force.

Then when the heart can wish no more,
With a strong couplet bars the door.

Scott was a friend of Christina Rossetti, who preferred Italian form and open doors, as have perhaps a majority of sonneteers. But all poems have to end somehow, and the generally different tone and direction of Italian and English endings may be freely observed in this volume. Here are some random examples of a selection of effects, which the reader may wish to consult at leisure.

In the Italian sonnet, the sinewy deployment of the tercets contrives a paced concentration, with suspension of description or attainment of a tableau (99, 103, 118, 140, 239, 276), intensification of the situation or emotion (79, 86, 111, 154, 173, 226, 235, 267, 305), acceleration of proof or clarifying explanation (77, 102, 113, 137, 150, 185, 278), fresh re-entry into the problem (198, 246, 288, 302), pure suggestiveness (141, 163, 176, 240, 297, 321), open questions (217, 247, 274), questions that assert what they question (106, 164, 299), containment (144, 242, 251), and expansion (158,

179, 182, 227, 287, 301). By sufficient contrast, the conduct of the couplet in the English sonnet enables triumphant conclusion (55, 61, 123, 262, 265, 271), simple summary (9, 36, 66, 100, 116, 119, 165, 207, 282, 286, 304), the aphorism that forbids further reflection (41, 70, 115, 268, 273), paradox (1, 32, 145, 215, 244, 254, 280, 296, 323), challenge (42, 303, 308, 318), and reversal (33, 71, 149, 258, 293, 313). This is, of course, an approximate indication of characteristics and not an inflexible set of distinctions. After the Romantic period, when an Italian octave and an English sestet became frequent, and when there was wide experimentation with rhyme-schemes, with much enjambement and overrunning of quatrains and tercets, these characteristics become less predictable.

3

In making my choice here of sonnets in English from Wyatt to the present day, I have chosen to be, or have found myself, confined in certain respects that should eventually be clear enough to the involved reader. I had no intention of representing foreign sonnets, and thus in the main have avoided translations. However, the very first sonnet is fully indebted to Petrarch, and echoes of other early sonneteers are everywhere. I have also introduced a translation of one of Milton's sonnets from the Italian, believing it to represent a significant element in his achievement. I have tended to be conservative in representing deviations from the basic types of sonnet, although the reader will find a number of common and less common variants, including the inverted sonnet (Brooke) and the iterating sonnet (Wroth, Leigh Hunt). The unrhymed sonnet, which goes back at least to Spenser, is so common in the present day with our mistrust of rhyme (and

widespread unwillingness to handle it) that I have very few exam-
ples (e.g. Darley; and from recent years, Ewart and Armitage). I
have some sonnets in tetrameters (e.g. Carew, Waller, Merrill) but
none in shorter lines. The special case of the quatorzain consisting
of seven couplets will be found here early and late (e.g. Behn and
Longley), but I have not included as many as I might have liked.
The difficulty is the pure defiance of sonnet structure that consec-
utive couplets encourage, and yet there is, I admit, a fine line to be
drawn between a set of seven couplets that carries itself like a
sonnet, and one that feels accidental (as, for instance, Anne
Bradstreet's account of the Persian monarchy, or, for that matter,
fourteen-line paragraphs in longer poems, such as Pope's cele-
brated passage 'Lo, the poor Indian . . .' in *An Essay on Man*). I have
not included 'sonnets' in other numbers of lines, since one can
soon reach the absurdity of concluding that something like
Tennyson's 'The Kraken' (fifteen lines) is 'really' a sonnet. In the
case of sequences, for which the sonnet has throughout its history
had an eminent use in larger symbolic structures, in coronas,
baroque double- or triple-coronas, sonnets of sonnets, and so on,
or in lyric commentary within prose works, it has been impossible
to be representative. I have, of course, included many sonnets
from sequences, but I have also included a corona by Chapman
and a fourteen-sonnet sequence by Christina Rossetti, as well as a
number of much shorter sets of sonnets (including Shelley's 'Ode
to the West Wind', which happily combines *terza rima* with sonnet
form). Consideration of publishing expense has limited the
number of sonnets included that are still within copyright. I have
given three each to a few poets who seem to me particularly to
deserve it (Robinson, Frost, Millay, and Auden) but after the last of
these there has necessarily been a ration of one each. This is hard

on poets such as Lowell, Merrill, Heaney, and Muldoon, who are all bountiful and in some cases innovating sonneteers.

Modernized spelling has been required for this anthology. I have therefore in the case of many of the earlier sonnets also taken the opportunity to make punctuation conform to present-day practice (we prefer lighter pointing). I have reduced capitalization unless distinct personification or significant absolutes are intended. I have expanded elisions that have no metrical force and added stress marks where these assist scansion. I have on occasion taken the liberty of making emendations (e.g. to distinguish the vocative 'O' from the exclamatory 'oh'). From the eighteenth century onwards one is likely to come across deliberate archaisms, such as the Miltonic past participle in –t, so I have been wary of over-modernizing. I have benefited from Stanley Wells's discussion of many of these issues in his *Modernizing Shakespeare's Spelling* (1979), but any errors of judgement which readers may observe are all my own. I have not always taken my texts from the earliest editions by any means, and I have frequently used reprints and modern editions, as will be clear from the section 'Sources and Notes', where will also be found some minimal explanatory commentary.

JOHN FULLER

THE
OXFORD BOOK OF
Sonnets

1   *'Whoso list to hunt, I know where is an hind'*

WHOSO list to hunt, I know where is an hind,
   But as for me, alas, I may no more.
   The vain travail hath wearied me so sore,
   I am of them that farthest cometh behind.
Yet may I by no means my wearied mind
   Draw from the deer, but as she fleeth afore
Fainting I follow. I leave off therefore,
   Since in a net I seek to hold the wind.
Who list her hunt, I put him out of doubt
   As well as I may spend his time in vain;
   And, graven with diamonds, in letters plain
There is written her fair neck round about:
   Noli me tangere, for Caesar's I am,
   And wild for to hold, though I seem tame.

SIR THOMAS WYATT

2 *'Farewell, Love, and all thy laws for ever'*

FAREWELL, Love, and all thy laws for ever:
    Thy baited hooks shall tangle me no more.
    Senec and Plato call me from thy lore
    To perfect wealth my wit for to endeavour.
In blind error when I did persever,
    Thy sharp repulse that pricketh ay so sore
    Hath taught me to set in trifles no store
    And scape forth, since liberty is lever.
Therefore, farewell: go trouble younger hearts
    And in me claim no more authority.
    With idle youth go use thy property
And thereon spend thy many brittle darts,
    For hitherto though I have lost all my time
    Me lusteth no longer rotten boughs to climb.

SIR THOMAS WYATT

3   *'Unstable dream, according to the place'*

UNSTABLE dream, according to the place
   Be steadfast once, or else at least be true.
   By tasted sweetness make me not to rue
   The sudden loss of thy false feignèd grace.
By good respect in such a dangerous case
   Thou broughtest not her into this tossing mew
   But madest my sprite live my care to renew,
   My body in tempest her succour to embrace.
The body dead, the sprite had his desire.
   Painless was th'one, th'other in delight.
   Why then, alas, did it not keep it right,
Returning to leap into the fire,
   And where it was at wish it could not remain?
   Such mocks of dreams they turn to deadly pain.

SIR THOMAS WYATT

4   *'Set me whereas the sun doth parch the green'*

SET me whereas the sun doth parch the green
Or where his beams may not dissolve the ice,
In temperate heat where he is felt and seen;
With proud people, in presence sad and wise;
Set me in base, or yet in high degree;
In the long night, or in the shortest day;
In clear weather, or where mists thickest be;
In lusty youth, or when my hairs be grey;
Set me in earth, in heaven, or yet in hell;
In hill, in dale, or in the foaming flood;
Thrall, or at large, alive whereso I dwell;
Sick, or in health; in ill fame or in good.
  Yours will I be, and with that only thought
  Comfort myself when that my hap is nought.

HENRY HOWARD, EARL OF SURREY

5 'Norfolk sprang thee, Lambeth holds thee dead'

NORFOLK sprang thee, Lambeth holds thee dead,
Clere, of the County of Cleremont, though hight.
Within the womb of Ormond's race thou bred,
And sawest thy cousin crownèd in thy sight.
Shelton for love, Surrey for Lord, thou chase;—
Ay me! while life did last that league was tender,
Tracing whose steps thou sawest Kelsall blaze,
Laundersey burnt, and battered Bullen render.
At Muttrel gates, hopeless of all recure,
Thine Earl, half dead, gave in thy hand his will,
Which cause did thee this pining death procure,
Ere summers four times seven thou could'st fulfil.
    Ah, Clere! if love had booted, care, or cost,
    Heaven had not won, nor earth so timely lost.

HENRY HOWARD, EARL OF SURREY

6 *'I saw, sweet Licia, when the spider ran'*

I SAW, sweet Licia, when the spider ran
Within your house to weave a worthless web.
You present were and feared her with your fan,
So that amazèd, speedily she fled.
She in your house such sweet perfumes did smell,
And heard the Muses, with their notes refined.
Thus filled with envy, could no longer dwell,
But straight returned, and at your house repined.
Then tell me, spider, why of late I saw
Thee loose thy poison, and thy bowels gone:
Did these enchant and keep thy limbs in awe,
And made thy forces to be small or none?
   No, no, thou didst by chance my Licia see,
   Who, for her look, Minerva seemed to thee.

GILES FLETCHER

7   'More than most fair, full of the living fire'

MORE than most fair, full of the living fire,
   Kindled above unto the maker near,
   No eyes but joys, in which all powers conspire
   That to the world naught less be counted dear,
Through your bright beams doth not the blinded guest
   Shoot out his darts to base affections wound?
   But angels come to lead frail minds to rest
   In chaste desires on heavenly beauty bound.
You frame my thoughts and fashion me within,
   You stop my tongue and teach my heart to speak,
   You calm the storm that passion did begin,
   Strong through your cause, but by your virtue weak.
Dark is the world where your light shinèd never;
   Well is he born that may behold you ever.

EDMUND SPENSER

8 *'Sweet warrior, when shall I have peace with you?'*

❦❦❦

SWEET warrior, when shall I have peace with you?
   High time it is this war now ended were,
   Which I no longer can endure to sue,
   Nor your incessant battery more to bear.
So weak my powers, so sore my wounds appear,
   That wonder is how I should live a jot,
   Seeing my heart through-launchèd everywhere
   With thousand arrows, which your eyes have shot.
Yet shoot ye sharply still and spare me not,
   But glory think to make these cruel stours.
   Ye cruel one, what glory can be got
   In slaying him that would live gladly yours?
Make peace therefore, and grant me timely grace
   That all my wounds will heal in little space.

EDMUND SPENSER

9   *'Coming to kiss her lips, such grace I found'*

Coming to kiss her lips, such grace I found
    Me seemed I smelled a garden of sweet flowers,
    That dainty odours from them threw around
    For damsels fit to deck their lovers' bowers.
Her lips did smell like unto gillyflowers,
    Her ruddy cheeks like unto roses red,
    Her snowy brows like budded belamours,
    Her lovely eyes like pinks but newly spread,
Her goodly bosom like a strawberry bed,
    Her neck like to a bunch of columbines,
    Her breast like lilies, ere their leaves be shed,
    Her nipples like young blossomed jessamines.
Such fragrant flowers do give most odorous smell,
    But her sweet odour did them all excell.

EDMUND SPENSER

10   *'One day I wrote her name upon the strand'*

ONE day I wrote her name upon the strand,
    But came the waves and washèd it away.
    Again I wrote it with a second hand,
    But came the tide and made my pains his prey.
'Vain man', said she, 'that dost in vain assay
    A mortal thing so to immortalize,
    For I myself shall like to this decay
    And eke my name be wipèd out likewise.'
Not so,' quoth I, 'let baser things devise
    To die in dust, but you shall live by fame.
    My verse your virtues rare shall eternise
    And in the heavens write your glorious name,
Where, whenas death shall all the world subdue,
    Our love shall live, and later life renew.

EDMUND SPENSER

11 *'Was it a dream, or did I see it plain'*

❦❦❦

Was it a dream, or did I see it plain,
    A goodly table of pure ivory,
    All spread with junkets, fit to entertain
    The greatest prince with pompous royalty?
'Mongst which, there in a silver dish did lie
    Two golden apples of unvalued price,
    Far passing those which Hercules came by,
    Or those which Atalanta did entice.
Exceeding sweet, yet void of sinful vice,
    That many sought, yet none could ever taste,
    Sweet fruit of pleasure brought from paradise
    By Love himself and in his garden placed.
Her breast that table was, so richly spread,
    My thoughts the guests, which would thereon have fed.

EDMUND SPENSER

12   *Sir Walter Ralegh to his son*

THREE things there be that prosper up apace
And flourish, whilst they grow asunder far,
But on a day they meet all in one place
And when they meet they one another mar,
And they be these: the wood, the weed, the wag.
The wood is that which makes the gallow-tree,
The weed is that which strings the hangman's bag,
The wag, my pretty knave, betokeneth thee.
Mark well, dear boy, whilst these assemble not,
Green springs the tree, hemp grows, the wag is wild,
But when they meet it makes the timber rot,
It frets the halter and it chokes the child.
    Then bless thee, and beware, and let us pray
    We part not with thee at this meeting day.

SIR WALTER RALEGH

13   *'Satan, no woman, yet a wandering spirit'*

SATAN, no woman, yet a wandering spirit,
When he saw ships sail two ways with one wind,
Of sailor's trade he hell did disinherit:
The Devil himself loves not a half-fast mind.

The satyr when he saw the shepherd blow
To warm his hands, and make his pottage cool,
Manhood forswears, and half a beast did know
Nature with double breath is put to school.

Cupid doth head his shafts in women's faces,
Where smiles and tears dwell ever near together,
Where all the arts of change give passion graces.
While these clouds threaten, who fears not the weather?
  Sailors and satyrs, Cupid's knights, and I,
    Fear women that swear, Nay; and know they lie.

FULKE GREVILLE, LORD BROOKE

14   *'Loving in truth, and fain in verse
my love to show'*

LOVING in truth, and fain in verse my love to show,
That the dear she might take some pleasure of my pain,
Pleasure might cause her read, reading might make her know,
Knowledge might pity win, and pity grace obtain,
    I sought fit words to paint the blackest face of woe,
Studying inventions fine, her wits to entertain,
Oft turning others' leaves to see if thence would flow
Some fresh and fruitful showers upon my sunburned brain.
    But words came halting forth, wanting Invention's stay.
Invention, Nature's child, fled step-dame Study's blows,
And others' feet still seemed but strangers in my way.
Thus great with child to speak, and helpless in my throes,
    Biting my truant pen, beating myself for spite,
    'Fool,' said my Muse to me, 'look in thy heart and write.'

SIR PHILIP SIDNEY

15　*'In truth, O Love, with what a boyish kind'*

In truth, O Love, with what a boyish kind
　　Thou dost proceed in thy most serious ways,
　　That when the heaven to thee his best displays
Yet of that best thou leav'st the best behind.
For like a child that some fair book doth find,
　　With gilded leaves or coloured vellum plays
　　Or at the most on some fine picture stays,
But never heeds the fruit of writer's mind,
　　So when thou saw'st in Nature's cabinet
Stella, thou straight look'st babies in her eyes.
In her cheek's pit thou didst thy pitfall set
And in her breast bo-peep or couching lies,
　　Playing and shining in each outward part,
　　But, fool, seek'st not to get into her heart.

SIR PHILIP SIDNEY

16   *'With how sad steps, O moon,*
       thou climb'st the skies'

❧❧❧

WITH how sad steps, O moon, thou climb'st the skies,
  How silently, and with how wan a face.
  What, may it be that even in heavenly place
That busy archer his sharp arrows tries?
Sure, if that long with love acquainted eyes
  Can judge of love, thou feels a lover's case.
  I read it in thy looks; thy languished grace,
To me that feel the like, thy state descries.
  Then ev'n of fellowship, O moon, tell me
Is constant love deemed there but want of wit?
Are beauties there as proud as here they be?
Do they above love to be loved, and yet
  Those lovers scorn whom that love doth possess?
  Do they call virtue there ungratefulness?

SIR PHILIP SIDNEY

17   ## *'Come, sleep, O sleep, the certain knot of peace'*

❧❦❧❦

COME, sleep, O sleep, the certain knot of peace,
The baiting place of wit, the balm of woe,
The poor man's wealth, the prisoner's release,
The indifferent judge between the high and low,
     With shield of proof shield me from out the press
Of those fierce darts despair at me doth throw.
O make in me those civil wars to cease;
I will good tribute pay if thou do so.
     Take thou of me smooth pillows, sweetest bed,
A chamber deaf to noise and blind to light;
A rosy garland and a weary head;
And if these things, as being thine by right,
     Move not thy heavy grace, thou shalt in me,
     Livelier than elsewhere, Stella's image see.

SIR PHILIP SIDNEY

18 *'O kiss, which dost those ruddy gems impart'*

O KISS, which dost those ruddy gems impart,
Or gems, or fruits of new-found Paradise,
Breathing all bliss and sweetening to the heart,
Teaching dumb lips a nobler exercise.
   O kiss, which souls, even souls together ties
By links of love and only nature's art,
How fain would I paint thee to all men's eyes,
Or of thy gifts at least shade out some part.
   But she forbids, with blushing words; she says
   She builds her fame on higher-seated praise.
But my heart burns, I cannot silent be.
   Then since, dear life, you fain would have me peace,
   And I, mad with delight, want wit to cease,
Stop you my mouth with still still kissing me.

SIR PHILIP SIDNEY

19   *'Yourself the sun, and I the melting frost'*

YOURSELF the sun, and I the melting frost,
    Myself the flax and you the kindling fire,
Yourself the maze wherein my self is lost,
    I your disdain, yet you my heart's desire,
Your love the port whereto my fancies sail,
    My hope the ship whose helm your fair hand guides,
Your grace the wind that must my course avail,
    My faith the flood, your frowns the ebbing tides,
Yourself the spring and I the leafless tree,
    Myself the bird, the closèd cage your breast,
You are the flower and I the toiling bee.
    My thoughts in you, though yours elsewhere, do rest.
You are the brook and I the deer embossed.
My heaven is you, yet you torment my ghost.

SIR ARTHUR GORGES

21

20–9 *A Coronet for his Mistress Philosophy*

❦ i ❦

MUSES that sing love's sensual empery,
    And lovers kindling your enragèd fires
    At Cupid's bonfires burning in the eye,
    Blown with the empty breath of vain desires,
You that prefer the painted cabinet
    Before the wealthy jewels it doth store ye,
    That all your joys in dying figures set,
    And stain the living substance of your glory,
Abjure those joys, abhor their memory,
    And let my love the honoured subject be
    Of love, and honour's complete history.
    Your eyes were never yet let in to see
The majesty and riches of the mind,
But dwell in darkness, for your god is blind.

❦ ii ❦

BUT dwell in darkness, for your god is blind.
   Humour pours down such torrents on his eyes,
   Which, as from mountains, fall on his base kind
   And eat your entrails out with ecstasies.
Colour, whose hands for faintness are not felt,
   Can bind your waven thoughts in adamant
   And with her painted fires your hearts doth melt,
   Which beat your souls in pieces with a pant.
But my love is the cordial of souls,
   Teaching by passion what perfection is,
   In whose fixed beauties shine the sacred scrolls
   And long-lost records of your human bliss,
Spirit to flesh and soul to spirit giving.
Love flows not from my liver, but her living.

❧❧❧ iii ❧❧❧

Love flows not from my liver but her living,
    From whence all stings to perfect love are darted,
    All power and thought of prideful lust depriving,
    Her life so pure and she so spotless-hearted,
In whom sits beauty with so firm a brow
    That age, nor care, nor torment can contract it.
    Heaven's glories shining there do stuff allow
    And virtue's constant graces do compact it.
Her mind, the beam of God, draws in the fires
    Of her chaste eyes, from all earth's tempting fuel,
    Which upward lifts the looks of her desires
    And makes each precious thought in her a jewel,
And as huge fires compressed more proudly flame
So her close beauties further blaze her fame.

iv

So her close beauties further blaze her fame,
    When from the world into herself reflected
    She lets her shameless glory in her shame,
    Content for heaven to be of earth rejected.
She, thus depressed, knocks at Olympus' gate,
    And in th'untainted temple of her heart
    Doth the divorceless nuptials celebrate
    'Twixt God and her, where love's prophanèd dart
Feeds the chaste flames of Hymen's firmament,
    Wherein she sacrificeth, for her part,
    The robes, looks, deeds, desires and whole descent
    Of female natures built in shops of art.
Virtue is both the merit and reward
Of her removed and soul-infused regard.

❦❦❦ V ❦❦❦

OF her removed and soul-infused regard,
    With whose firm species, as with golden lances,
    She points her life's field, for all wars prepared,
    And bears one chanceless mind in all mischances.
Th'inversèd world that goes upon her head
    And with her wanton heels doth kick the sky
    My love disdains, though she be honourèd
    And without envy sees her empery,
Loathes all her toys and thoughts cupidinine,
    Arranging in the army of her face
    All virtue's forces to dismay loose eyen
    That hold no quarter with renown or grace.
War to all frailty, peace of all things pure
Her look doth promise and her life assure.

❧❧❧ vi ❧❧❧

HER look doth promise and her life assure
  A right line, forcing a rebateless point
  In her high deeds through everything obscure
  To full perfection. Not the weak disjoint
Of female humours, nor the Protean rages
  Of pied-faced fashion that doth shrink and swell,
  Working poor men like waxen images
  And makes them apish strangers where they dwell,
Can alter her. Titles of primacy,
  Courtship of antic gestures, brainless jests,
  Blood without soul of false nobility,
  Nor any folly that the world infests
Can alter her who with her constant guises
To living virtues turns the deadly vices.

◆◇◆ vii ◆◇◆

To living virtues turns the deadly vices,
    For covetous she is of all good parts:
    Incontinent, for still she shows entices
    To consort with them, sucking out their hearts;
Proud, for she scorns prostrate humility,
    And gluttonous in store of abstinence;
    Drunk with extractions stilled in fervency
    From contemplation and true continence;
Burning in wrath against impatience
    And sloth itself, for she will never rise
    From that all-seeing trance, the band of sense,
    Wherein in view of all souls' skilled she lies.
No constancy to that her mind doth move,
Nor riches to the virtues of my love.

❧❧❧ viii ❧❧❧

Nor riches to the virtues of my love,
    Nor empire to her mighty government,
    Which fair analysed in her beauty's grove
    Shows laws for care and canons for content.
And as a purple tincture given to glass
    By clear transmission of the sun doth taint
    Opposèd subjects, so my mistress' face
    Doth reverence in her viewers' brows depaint,
And, like the pansy, with a little veil
    She gives her inward work the greater grace,
    Which my lines imitate, though much they fail,
    Her gifts so high and time's conceits so base.
Her virtues then above my verse must raise her,
For words want art and art wants words to praise her.

❧❧❧ ix ❧❧❧

FOR words want art and art wants words to praise her,
    Yet shall my active and industrious pen
    Wind his sharp forehead through those parts that saise her,
    And register her worth past rarest women.
Herself shall be my muse, that well will know
    Her proper inspirations and assuage
    With her dear love the wrongs my fortunes show,
    Which to my youth bind heartless grief in age.
Herself shall be my comfort and my riches,
    And all my thoughts I will on her convert.
    Honour, and error, which the world bewitches,
    Shall still crown fools and tread upon desert,
And never shall my friendless verse envy
Muses that fame's loose feathers beautify.

❧❧❧ X ❧❧❧

MUSES that fame's loose feathers beautify,
   And such as scorn to tread the theatre,
   As ignorant, the seed of memory
   Have most inspired and shown their glories there
To noblest wits and men of highest doom
   That for the kingly laurel bent affair.
   The theatres of Athens and Rome
   Have been the crowns and not the base impair.
Far then be this foul cloudy-brow'd contempt
   From like-plumed birds, and let your sacred rhymes
   From honour's court their servile feet exempt
   That live by soothing moods and serving times.
And let my love adorn with modest eyes
Muses that sing love's sensual emperies.

Lucidius olim.

GEORGE CHAPMAN

30   *'Uncivil sickness, hast thou no regard'*

UNCIVIL sickness, hast thou no regard
   But dost presume my dearest to molest,
   And without leave dar'st enter in that breast
   Whereto sweet love approach yet never dared?
Spare thou her health, which my life hath not spared.
   Too bitter such revenge of my unrest:
   Although with wrongs my thought she hath oppressed,
   My wrongs seek not revenge; they crave reward.
Cease, sickness, cease in her then to remain,
   And come and welcome, harbour thou in me,
   Whom love long since hath taught to suffer pain.
   So she which hath so oft my pains increased,
     (Oh God, that I might so rewarded be!)
     By my more pain might have her pain released.

HENRY CONSTABLE

31 *'Care-charmer sleep, son of the sable night'*

CARE-CHARMER sleep, son of the sable night,
   Brother to death, in silent darkness born,
   Relieve my languish and restore the light,
   With dark forgetting of my care's return.
And let the day be time enough to mourn
   The shipwreck of my ill-adventured youth.
   Let waking eyes suffice to wail their scorn
   Without the torment of the night's untruth.
Cease, dreams, th'imag'ry of our day-desires,
   To model forth the passions of the morrow.
   Never let rising sun approve you liars
   To add more grief to aggravate my sorrow.
Still let me sleep, embracing clouds in vain,
And never wake to feel the day's disdain.

SAMUEL DANIEL

32 *'You not alone, when you are still alone'*

You not alone, when you are still alone,
O God, from you that I could private be!
Since you one were, I never since was one,
Since you in me, myself since out of me,
Transported from myself into your being,
Though either distant, present yet to either,
Senseless with too much joy, each other seeing,
And only absent when we are together.
Give me myself and take yourself again.
Devise some means but how I may forsake you.
So much is mine that doth with you remain,
That taking what is mine, with me I take you.
    You do bewitch me. Oh that I could fly
    From myself you, or from your own self I.

MICHAEL DRAYTON

33 *'Since there's no help, come let us kiss and part'*

SINCE there's no help, come let us kiss and part.
Nay, I have done: you get no more of me,
And I am glad, yea glad with all my heart
That thus so cleanly I myself can free.
Shake hands for ever, cancel all our vows,
And when we meet at any time again,
Be it not seen in either of our brows
That we one jot of former love retain.
Now at the last gasp of love's latest breath,
When, his pulse failing, passion speechless lies,
When faith is kneeling by his bed of death
And innocence is closing up his eyes,
    Now, if thou would'st, when all have given him over,
    From death to life thou might'st him yet recover.

MICHAEL DRAYTON

34-5 *Acrostiteliostichon*

J f patience true could termine passions war R———
O ur thankefull Harpe had tendred long-ag O———
S ave that, our Griefs, whose deep-gulfs never eb B———
U nto you sacred, by the which you se E———
A h, muse not, then, if all our Muse-work savou R———
H eart sad, Art bad; yet pray you read the res T———
S o deare *Mecœnas*, if your patience daig N———
Y our praises due to publish farre and n I———
L ifting your Name, the glory of your Sto C———
V nthrall to Time, for, Time that tryeth s O———
E lse had th' old Hebrews and brave Worthies al L———
ST ones wear, steel wasts, too weak to bear their glorie S———
E ven so devout as wee are found to do O———
R ecording loftie though wee low begu N———

R are type of gentrie, and true Vertues Star R

O ne entire payment of the Zeale wee O

B reake still the best threades of our busie we B

E vill the Muses with griev'd mindes agre E

R uth, more then Youth, and rather cry than quave R

T is said of somethings, that the last is bes T

N o praise, but pardon to our new-found strai N

I will enforce my leaden Thoughts to fl I

C loude-high, to grave it, in a Diamond Ro C

O n every thing, forbeares the Muses th O

L ost with their lives, their Lives memorial L

S weet learning, yet, keeps fresh their famous storie S

O ur verse, your Vertues shall eternize to O

N othing a whit more cleare then radiant Su N

JOSHUA SYLVESTER

37

36   *'Shall I compare thee to a summer's day?'*

SHALL I compare thee to a summer's day?
Thou art more lovely and more temperate:
Rough winds do shake the darling buds of May,
And summer's lease hath all too short a date:
Sometime too hot the eye of heaven shines,
And often is his gold complexion dimmed,
And every fair from fair sometime declines,
By chance, or nature's changing course untrimmed:
But thy eternal summer shall not fade,
Nor lose possession of that fair thou ow'st,
Nor shall death brag thou wand'rest in his shade,
When in eternal lines to time thou grow'st,
    So long as men can breath or eyes can see,
    So long lives this, and this gives life to thee.

WILLIAM SHAKESPEARE

37   *'Not marble, nor the gilded monuments'*

NOT marble, nor the gilded monuments
Of princes shall outlive this powerful rhyme,
But you shall shine more bright in these contents
Than unswept stone, besmeared with sluttish time.
When wasteful war shall statues overturn,
And broils root out the work of masonry,
Nor Mars his sword, nor war's quick fire, shall burn
The living record of your memory.
'Gainst death, and all oblivious enmity
Shall you pace forth, your praise shall still find room,
Even in the eyes of all posterity
That wear this world out to the ending doom.
    So till the judgement that yourself arise,
        You live in this, and dwell in lovers' eyes.

WILLIAM SHAKESPEARE

38 *'Like as the waves make towards the*
pebbled shore'

❦❦❦

LIKE as the waves make towards the pebbled shore,
So do our minutes hasten to their end,
Each changing place with that which goes before,
In sequent toil all forwards do contend.
Nativity, once in the main of light,
Crawls to maturity, wherewith being crowned,
Crooked eclipses 'gainst his glory fight,
And time that gave doth now his gift confound.
Time doth transfix the flourish set on youth,
And delves the parallels in beauty's brow,
Feeds on the rarities of nature's truth,
And nothing stands but for his scythe to mow.
    And yet to times in hope my verse shall stand
    Praising thy worth, despite his cruel hand.

WILLIAM SHAKESPEARE

39   *'Since brass, nor stone, nor earth,*
       nor boundless sea'

SINCE brass, nor stone, nor earth, nor boundless sea,
But sad mortality o'ersways their power,
How with this rage shall beauty hold a plea,
Whose action is no stronger than a flower?
O how shall summer's honey breath hold out,
Against the wrackful siege of batt'ring days,
When rocks impregnable are not so stout,
Nor gates of steel so strong but time decays?
O fearful meditation, where alack,
Shall time's best jewel from time's chest lie hid?
Or what strong hand can hold his swift foot back,
Or who his spoil o'er beauty can forbid?
    O none, unless this miracle have might,
    That in black ink my love may still shine bright.

WILLIAM SHAKESPEARE

40 *'That time of year thou mayst in me behold'*

THAT time of year thou mayst in me behold,
When yellow leaves, or none, or few do hang
Upon those boughs which shake against the cold,
Bare ruined choirs, where late the sweet birds sang.
In me thou seest the twilight of such day,
As after sunset fadeth in the west,
Which by and by black night doth take away,
Death's second self that seals up all in rest.
In me thou seest the glowing of such fire,
That on the ashes of his youth doth lie,
As the death-bed whereon it must expire,
Consumed with that which it was nourished by.
    This thou perceiv'st, which makes thy love more strong,
    To love that well which thou must leave ere long.

WILLIAM SHAKESPEARE

41   *'They that have power to hurt,
and will do none'*

THEY that have power to hurt, and will do none,
That do not do the thing they most do show,
Who, moving others, are themselves as stone,
Unmovèd, cold, and to temptation slow:
They rightly do inherit heaven's graces,
And husband nature's riches from expense,
They are the lords and owners of their faces,
Others but stewards of their excellence:
The summer's flower is to the summer sweet,
Though to it self, it only live and die,
But if that flower with base infection meet,
The basest weed outbraves his dignity:
    For sweetest things turn sourest by their deeds;
    Lilies that fester smell far worse than weeds.

WILLIAM SHAKESPEARE

42   *'Let me not to the marriage of true minds'*

LET me not to the marriage of true minds
Admit impediments. Love is not love
Which alters when it alteration finds,
Or bends with the remover to remove.
O no, it is an ever-fixèd mark
That looks on tempests and is never shaken;
It is the star to every wand'ring bark,
Whose worth's unknown, although his height be taken.
Love's not time's fool, though rosy lips and cheeks
Within his bending sickle's compass come.
Love alters not with his brief hours and weeks,
But bears it out even to the edge of doom.
　　If this be error and upon me proved,
　　I never writ, nor no man ever loved.

WILLIAM SHAKESPEARE

43   *'Two loves I have of comfort and despair'*

Two loves I have of comfort and despair,
Which like two spirits do suggest me still.
The better angel is a man right fair,
The worser spirit a woman coloured ill.
To win me soon to hell my female evil
Tempteth my better angel from my side,
And would corrupt my saint to be a devil,
Wooing his purity with her foul pride.
And whether that my angel be turned fiend,
Suspect I may, yet not directly tell,
But being both from me both to each friend,
I guess one angel in another's hell.
    Yet this shall I ne'er know but live in doubt,
    Till my bad angel fire my good one out.

WILLIAM SHAKESPEARE

44   *'When first I learned the ABC of love'*

WHEN first I learned the ABC of love,
I was unapt to learn, and since a cross
Crossed my way to them, I was loath to prove
That learning that might tend but to my loss.
The vowels (looks) that spelled mute consonants
I hardly could distinguish what they were.
And since the rest to them were dissonants,
To make them join with vowels cost me dear!
The mutes and consonants, being deeds and words,
Were harsh without sweet vowels (sweetest looks).
My youth was spent, for age such skill affords,
Ere them I knew with, and without, my books.
    But (tears) the liquids, still being in my eyes,
    I saw through them, at last, love's mysteries.

JOHN DAVIES OF HEREFORD

45 *'It is as true as strange, else trial feigns'*

I T is as true as strange, else trial feigns,
That whosoever in the moonshine sleeps
Are hardly waked, the moon so rules the brains.
For she is sovereign of the brains and deeps:
So thou, fair Cynthia, with thy borrowed beams,
(Borrowed of glory's sun, great lord of light!)
Mak'st me still sleep, in love, whose golden dreams
Give love right current, since well-coined, delight.
I cannot wake, while thou on me dost shine,
Thy shining so, makes me so sweetly dream.
For still, methinks, I kiss those lips of thine
And,—nothing else, for I will not blaspheme.
　　But thought is free, and dreams are dreams, and so
　　I dream, and dream, and dream, but let that go.

JOHN DAVIES OF HEREFORD

46 'Give me, fair sweet, the map, well-colourèd'

GIVE me, fair sweet, the map, well-colourèd,
Of that same little world, yourself, to see
Whether those zones of hot love and cold dread
Be so extreme in you as th'are in me.
If on the heart (that small world's centre great)
Such heat and cold their utmost powers employ,
No thoughts could dwell therein for cold and heat,
Which my distempered-dismal thoughts annoy.
But if I find the climes more temperate
In your world than in mine, I'll thither send
My thoughts by colonies, in wretched state,
Since there, forthwith, they cannot choose but mend:
    And by your temperance, when they bettered be,
    If you'll transplant them, them replant in me.

JOHN DAVIES OF HEREFORD

47 'So shoots a star as doth my mistress glide'

So shoots a star as doth my mistress glide
At midnight through my chamber; which she makes
Bright as the sky, when moon and stars are spied,
Wherewith my sleeping eyes, amazèd, wake.
Which ope no sooner than herself she shuts
Out of my sight, away so fast she flies,
Which me in mind of my slack service puts,
For which all night I wake, to plague mine eyes.
Shoot, star, once more! and if I be thy mark
Thou shalt hit me, for thee I'll meet withal.
Let mine eyes once more see thee in the dark,
Else they, with ceaseless waking, out will fall.
    And if again such time and place I lose,
    To close with thee, let mine eyes never close.

JOHN DAVIES OF HEREFORD

48 *'Thrice toss these oaken ashes in the air'*

THRICE toss these oaken ashes in the air,
And thrice three times tie up this true-love's knot.
Thrice sit thee down in this enchanted chair
And murmur soft, she will or she will not.
Go burn these poisoned weeds in that blue fire,
This cypress gathered at a dead man's grave,
These screech-owl's feathers and this pricking briar,
That all thy thorny cares an end may have.
Then come, you fairies, dance with me a round.
Dance in this circle, let my love be centre,
Melodiously breathe out a charming sound.
Melt her hard heart, that some remorse may enter.
    In vain are all the charms I can devise,
     She hath an art to break them with her eyes.

THOMAS CAMPION

49 'Lo here I am, lord, whither wilt thou send me?'

Lo here I am, lord, whither wilt thou send me?
To which part of my soul, which region?
Whether the palace of my whole dominion,
My mind? which doth not rightly apprehend thee,
And needs more light of knowledge to amend me;
Or to the parliamental session,
My will? that doth design all action,
And doth not as it ought attend thee,
But suffers sin and pleasures, which offend thee,
Within thy kingdom to continue faction;
Or to my heart's great lordship shall I bend me,
Where love, the steward of affection,
On vain and barren pleasures doth dispend me?
Lord I am here, O give me thy commission.

WILLIAM ALABASTER

50   *'Dear, and so worthy both by your desert'*

≈❀≈❀≈

DEAR, and so worthy both by your desert
Enlarged to me, and those favours rare
Of nature and of grace which in you are,
Accept the counsel of unfalsèd heart,
Which to myself in you I do impart,
Upon your soul to take severer care,
How to assure it of eternal welfare,
And cut off the entail of endless smart.
Let us upon our mother's bosom rest,
Our Mother Church, from whose undried breast
The fairies after baptism did us steal,
And starvèd us with their enchanted bread.
Our mother of Christ's treasure hath the seal,
And with sweet junkets doth her table spread.

WILLIAM ALABASTER

51 '*Jove for Europa's love took shape of bull*'

JOVE for Europa's love took shape of bull,
    And for Calisto played Diana's part,
    And in a golden shower he filled full
    The lap of Danae with celestial art.
Would I were changed but to my mistress' gloves,
    That those white lovely fingers I might hide,
    That I might kiss those hands which mine heart loves,
    Or else that chain of pearl, her neck's vain pride,
Made proud with her neck's veins, that I might fold
    About that lovely neck and her paps tickle,
    Or her to compass like a belt of gold,
Or that sweet wine, which down her throat doth trickle,
    To kiss her lips and lie next at her heart,
    Run through her veins and pass by pleasure's part.

BARNABE BARNES

52 'The sacred muse that first made love divine'

THE sacred muse that first made love divine
Hath made him naked and without attire,
But I will clothe him with this pen of mine
That all the world his fashion shall admire:
His hat of hope, his band of beauty fine,
His cloak of craft, his doublet of desire;
Grief for a girdle shall about him twine;
His points of pride, his eyelet-holes of ire,
His hose of hate, his codpiece of conceit,
His stockings of stern strife, his shirt of shame,
His garters of vainglory, gay and slight,
His pantoufles of passions I will frame;
Pumps of presumption shall adorn his feet
And socks of sullenness exceeding sweet.

SIR JOHN DAVIES

53   *'I am a little world made cunningly'*

I AM a little world made cunningly
Of elements and an angelic sprite,
But black sin hath betrayed to endless night
My world's both parts, and oh, both parts must die!
You which beyond that heaven which was most high
Have found new spheres, and of new lands can write,
Pour new seas in mine eyes, that so I might
Drown my world with my weeping earnestly,
Or wash it, if it must be drowned no more.
But oh, it must be burnt! alas, the fire
Of lust and envy have burnt it heretofore,
And made it fouler. Let their flames retire,
And burn me, O Lord, with a fiery zeal
Of thee'and thy house, which doth in eating heal.

JOHN DONNE

54 '*At the round earth's imagined corners, blow*'

AT the round earth's imagined corners, blow
Your trumpets, angels, and arise, arise
From death, you numberless infinities
Of souls, and to your scattered bodies go,
All whom the flood did, and fire shall o'erthrow,
All whom war, dearth, age, agues, tyrannies,
Despair, law, chance, hath slain, and you whose eyes
Shall behold God and never taste death's woe.
But let them sleep, Lord, and me mourn a space,
For, if above all these, my sins abound,
'Tis late to ask abundance of thy grace
When we are there; here on this lowly ground
Teach me how to repent, for that's as good
As if thou'hadst sealed my pardon with thy blood.

JOHN DONNE

55 *'Death, be not proud, though some have callèd thee'*

DEATH, be not proud, though some have callèd thee
Mighty and dreadful, for thou art not so,
For those whom thou think'st thou dost overthrow
Die not, poor death, nor yet canst thou kill me.
From rest and sleep, which by thy pictures be,
Much pleasure, then from thee much more must flow,
And soonest our best men with thee do go,
Rest of their bones, and soul's delivery.
Thou art slave to fate, chance, kings and desperate men,
And dost with poison, war and sickness dwell,
And poppy or charms can make us sleep as well,
And better than thy stroke. Why swell'st thou then?
One short sleep past, we wake eternally
And death shall be no more; death, thou shalt die.

JOHN DONNE

56   *'Batter my heart, three-personed God, for you'*

❧❧❧

BATTER my heart, three-personed God, for you
As yet but knock, breathe, shine, and seek to mend.
That I may rise and stand, o'erthrow me 'and bend
Your force to break, blow, burn and make me new.
I, like an usurped town, to'another due,
Labour to admit you, but oh, to no end
Reason, your viceroy in me, me should defend,
But is captived, and proves weak or untrue.
Yet dearly I love you, and would be loved fain,
But am betrothed unto your enemy.
Divorce me,'untie, or break that knot again,
Take me to you, imprison me, for I
Except you'enthrall me, never shall be free,
Nor ever chaste, except you ravish me.

JOHN DONNE

57 *'Show me, dear Christ, thy spouse,*
so bright and clear'

❦❦❦

Show me, dear Christ, thy spouse, so bright and clear.
What, is it she, which on the other shore
Goes richly painted? or which robbed and tore
Laments and mournes in Germany and here?
Sleeps she a thousand, then peeps up one year?
Is she self-truth and errs? Now new, now'outwore?
Doth she, and did she, and shall she evermore
On one, on seven, or on no hill appear?
Dwells she with us, or like adventuring knights
First travel we to seek and then make love?
Betray, kind husband, thy spouse to our sights,
And let mine amorous soul court thy mild dove,
Who is most true and pleasing to thee then
When she'is embraced and open to most men.

JOHN DONNE

58 *'Beauty and Majesty are fallen at odds'*

BEAUTY and Majesty are fallen at odds:
    Th'one claims his cheek, the other claims his chin.
    Then Virtue comes and puts her title in.
(Quoth she) I make him like th'immortal gods.
(Quoth Majesty) I own his looks, his brow.
    His lips, (quoth Love) his eyes, his fair is mine.
    And yet (quoth Majesty) he is not thine,
I mix disdain with love's congealèd snow.
Aye, but (quoth Love) his locks are mine, by right.
    His stately gait is mine (quoth Majesty),
    And mine (quoth Virtue) is his modesty.
Thus, as they strive about this heavenly wight,
    At last the other two to Virtue yield
    The lists of Love, fought in fair Beauty's field.

RICHARD BARNFIELD

59   *'You well-compacted groves, whose light and shade'*

❦❦❦❦

You well-compacted groves, whose light and shade,
   Mixed equally, produce nor heat nor cold,
   Either to burn the young or freeze the old,
But to one even temper being made,
Upon a green embroidering through each glade
   An airy silver and a sunny gold,
   So clothe the poorest that they do behold
Themselves in riches which can never fade.
   While the wind whistles and the birds do sing,
While your twigs clip and while the leaves do friss,
   While the fruit ripens which those trunks do bring,
   Senseless to all but love, do you not spring
Pleasure of such a kind, as truly is
A self-renewing vegetable bliss?

EDWARD, LORD HERBERT OF CHERBURY

60 *'Slide soft, fair Forth, and make a crystal plain'*

SLIDE soft, fair Forth, and make a crystal plain,
Cut your white locks, and on your foamy face
Let not a wrinkle be when you embrace
The boat that earth's perfections doth contain.
Winds, wonder, and through wond'ring hold your pace,
Or if that ye your hearts cannot restrain
From sending sighs, feeling a lover's case,
Sigh, and in her fair hair yourselves enchain.
Or take these sighs which absence makes arise
From my oppressèd breast, and fill the sails,
Or some sweet breath new brought from paradise.
The floods do smile, love o'er the winds prevails,
    And yet huge waves arise. The cause is this:
    The ocean strives with Forth the boat to kiss.

WILLIAM DRUMMOND

61   *'To spread the azure canopy of heaven'*

To spread the azure canopy of heaven
And spangle it all with sparks of burning gold,
To place this pond'rous globe of earth so even
That it should all and nought should it uphold,
With motions strange t'endue the planets seven
And Jove to make so mild and Mars so bold,
To temper what is moist, dry, hot, and cold
Of all their jars that sweet accords are given,
Lord, to thy wisdom's nought, nought to thy might.
But that thou should'st, thy glory laid aside,
Come basely in mortality to 'bide
And die for those deserved an endless night,
    A wonder is, so far above our wit
    That angels stand amazed to think on it.

WILLIAM DRUMMOND

62 *'How do I find my soul's extremest anguish'*

How do I find my soul's extremest anguish,
    With restless care my heart's eternal languish?
    Torments in life increasing still with anguish,
    Unquiet sleeps which breed my senses' languish.

Hope yet appears which somewhat helps my anguish
    And lends a spark of life to salve this languish,
    Breath to desire, and ease to foregone anguish,
    Balms but not cures to bitter-tasting languish.

Yet straight I feel hope proves but greater anguish,
    False in itself to me brings cruel languish.
    Could I not hope, I suffer might my anguish
    At least with lesser torture smart and languish.

For rebel hope I see thy smiles are anguish,
Both prince and subject of e'erlasting languish.

LADY MARY WROTH

63 *'My heart is lost. What can I now expect?'*

✤✤✤✤✤✤

My heart is lost. What can I now expect?
   An evening fair, after a drowsy day?
   Alas, fond fancy, this is not the way
   To cure a mourning heart or salve neglect.

They who should help do me and help reject,
   Embracing loose desires and wanton play,
   While wanton base delights do bear the sway,
   And impudency reigns without respect.

O Cupid, let thy mother know her shame!
   'Tis time for her to leave this youthful flame
   Which doth dishonour her, is age's blame
   And takes away the greatness of thy name.

Thou god of love, she only queen of lust,
Yet strives by weakening thee to be unjust.

LADY MARY WROTH

64   *'Late in the forest I did Cupid see'*

LATE in the forest I did Cupid see.
   Cold, wet and crying, he had lost his way,
   And being blind was farther like to stray,
   Which sight a kind compassion bred in me.

I kindly took and dried him, while that he,
   Poor child, complained he starvèd was with stay,
   And pined for want of his accustomed prey,
   For none in that wild place his host would be.

I glad was of his finding, thinking sure
   This service should my freedom still procure,
   And in my arms I took him then unharmed,

Carrying him safe unto a myrtle bower.
   But in the way he made me feel his power,
   Burning my heart who had him kindly warmed.

LADY MARY WROTH

65 *'Juno, still jealous of her husband Jove'*

JUNO, still jealous of her husband Jove,
    Descended from above on earth to try
    Whether she there could find his chosen love
    Which made him from the heavens so often fly.

Close by the place where I for shade did lie
    She chasing came, but when she saw me move,
    'Have you not seen this way,' said she, 'to hie
    One in whom virtue never ground did prove,

He in whom love doth breed to stir more hate,
    Courting a wanton nymph for his delight?
    His name is Jupiter, my lord by fate,
    Who for her leaves me, heav'n, his throne and light.'

'I saw him not,' said I, 'although here are
Many in whose hearts love hath made like war.'

LADY MARY WROTH

66   *'Down in a valley, by a forest's side'*

DOWN in a valley, by a forest's side,
Near where the crystal Thames rolls on her waves,
I saw a mushroom stand in haughty pride,
As if the lilies grew to be his slaves;
The gentle daisy, with her silver crown,
Worn in the breast of many a shepherd's lass;
The humble violet, that lowly down
Salutes the gay nymphs as they trimly pass:
These, with a many more, methought, complained
That Nature should those needless things produce,
Which not alone the sun from others gained
But turn it wholly to their proper use.
    I could not choose but grieve that Nature made
    So glorious flowers to live in such a shade.

WILLIAM BROWNE

67   *Redemption*

Having been tenant long to a rich lord,
 Not thriving, I resolvèd to be bold
 And make a suit unto him, to afford
A new small-rented lease, and cancel th'old.
In heaven at his manor I him sought:
 They told me there that he was lately gone
 About some land, which he had dearly bought
Long since on earth, to take possession.
I straight returned, and knowing his great birth
 Sought him accordingly in great resorts,
 In cities, theatres, gardens, parks and courts.
At length I heard a ragged noise and mirth
 Of thieves and murderers: there I him espied,
 Who straight 'Your suit is granted' said, and died.

GEORGE HERBERT

68

Prayer

Prayer the Church's banquet, angels' age,
    God's breath in man returning to his birth,
    The soul in paraphrase, heart in pilgrimage,
The Christian plummet sounding heav'n and earth;
Engine against th'Almighty, sinners' tower,
    Reversed thunder, Christ-side-piercing spear,
    The six-days world transposing in an hour,
A kind of tune, which all things hear and fear;
Softness, and peace, and joy, and love, and bliss,
    Exalted manna, gladness of the best,
    Heaven in ordinary, man well-dressed,
The milky way, the bird of paradise,
    Church bells beyond the stars heard, the soul's blood,
    The land of spices; something understood.

GEORGE HERBERT

69

To my Rival

HENCE vain intruder, haste away.
   Wash not with thy unhallowed brine
The footsteps of my Celia's shrine,
Nor on her purer altars lay
Thy empty words, accents that may
   Some looser dame to love incline.
   She must have offerings more divine,
Such pearly drops as youthful May
Scatters before the rising day,
   Such smooth soft language as each line
Might stroke an angry god, or stay
   Jove's thunder, make the hearers pine
With envy. Do this, thou shalt be
Servant to her, rival with me.

THOMAS CAREW

70

To Castara. Upon Beauty

CASTARA, see that dust the sportive wind
So wantons with. 'Tis happ'ly all you'll find
Left of some beauty. And how still it flies,
To trouble, as it did in life, our eyes.
O empty boast of flesh! Though our heirs gild
The far-fetch Phrigian marble, which shall build
A burden to our ashes, yet will death
Betray them to the sport of every breath.
Dost thou, poor relic of our frailty, still
Swell up with glory? Or is it thy skill
To mock weak man, whom every wind of praise
Into the air doth 'bove his centre raise?
    If so, mock on. And tell him that his lust
      To beauty's madness. For it courts but dust.

WILLIAM HABINGTON

71 *To the Moment last past*

O WHITHER dost thou fly? Cannot my vow
Entreat thee tarry? Thou wert here but now
And thou art gone, like ships which plough the sea
And leave no print for man to track their way.
O unseen wealth! who thee did husband can
Outvie the jewels of the ocean,
The mines of th'earth! One sigh well spent in thee
Had been a purchase for eternity!
We will not lose thee then. Castara, where
Shall we find out his hidden sepulchre?
And we'll revive him. Not the cruel stealth
Of fate shall rob us of so great a wealth.
  Undone in thrift! while we besought his stay,
  Ten of his fellow moments fled away.

WILLIAM HABINGTON

72

Love's Farewell

TREADING the path to nobler ends,
A long farewell to love I gave,
Resolved my country and my friends
All that remained of me should have.
And this resolve no mortal dame,
None but those eyes could have o'erthrown.
The nymph I dare not, need not name,
So high, so like herself alone.
Thus the tall oak, which now aspires
Above the fear of private fires,
Grown and designed for nobler use,
Not to make warm, but build the house,
Though from our meaner flames secure,
Must that which falls from heaven endure.

EDMUND WALLER

73   *To Charles Diodati*

CHARLES—and I say it wond'ring—thou must know
   That I, who once assumed a scornful air,
   And scoffed at love, am fallen in his snare,
(Full many an upright man has fallen so)
Yet think me not thus dazzled by the flow
   Of golden locks, or damask cheek; more rare
   The heart-felt beauties of my foreign fair;
A mien majestic, with dark brows that show
The tranquil lustre of a lofty mind;
   Words exquisite, of idioms more than one,
And song, whose fascinating pow'r might bind,
   And from her sphere draw down the lab'ring Moon,
With such fire-darting eyes, that should I fill
My ears with wax, she would inchant me still.

                              WILLIAM COWPER
                         (translating John Milton's Italian)

74 *When the Assault was Intended to the City*

CAPTAIN or colonel, or knight in arms,
　　Whose chance on these defenceless doors may seize,
　　If deed of honour did thee ever please,
　　Guard them, and him within protect from harms.
He can requite thee, for he knows the charms
　　That call fame on such gentle acts as these,
　　And he can spread thy name o'er lands and seas,
　　Whatever clime the sun's bright circle warms.
Lift not thy spear against the Muses' bower.
　　The great Emathian conqueror bid spare
　　The house of Pindarus, when temple and tower
Went to the ground. And the repeated air
　　Of sad Electra's poet had the power
　　To save th'Athenian walls from ruin bare.

JOHN MILTON

75   *'Lady, that in the prime of earliest youth'*

LADY, that in the prime of earliest youth
   Wisely hast shunned the broad way and the green,
   And with those few art eminently seen
   That labour up the hill of heavenly truth,
The better part with Mary and with Ruth
   Chosen thou hast, and they that overween
   And at thy growing virtues fret their spleen
   No anger find in thee, but pity and ruth.
Thy care is fixed, and zealously attends
   To fill thy odorous lamp with deeds of light
   And hope that reaps not shame. Therefore be sure
Thou, when the bridegroom with his feastful friends
   Passes to bliss at the mid hour of night,
   Hast gained thy entrance, virgin wise and pure.

JOHN MILTON

76   *'A book was writ of late called*
Tetrachordon'

✧❀✧❀✧❀

A BOOK was writ of late called *Tetrachordon*,
   And woven close, both matter, form and style,
   The subject new. It walked the town awhile,
   Numb'ring good intellects, now seldom pored on.
Cries the stall-reader, 'Bless us! What a word on
   A title-page is this!' And some in file
   Stand spelling false, while one might walk to Mile-
   End Green. Why is it harder, sirs, than Gordon,
Colkitto, or Macdonnel, or Galasp?
   Those rugged names to our like mouths grow sleek
   That would have made Quintilian stare and gasp.
Thy age, like ours, O soul of Sir John Cheke,
   Hated not learning worse than toad or asp,
   When thou taught'st Cambridge and King Edward Greek.

JOHN MILTON

77 ## *On the late Massacre in Piedmont*

AVENGE, O Lord, thy slaughtered saints, whose bones
   Lie scattered on the Alpine mountains cold,
   Ev'n them who kept thy truth so pure of old
   When all our fathers worshipped stocks and stones,
Forget not. In thy book record their groans
   Who were thy sheep and in their ancient fold
   Slain by the bloody Piedmontese that rolled
   Mother with infant down the rocks. Their moans
The Vales redoubled to the hills, and they
   To heav'n. Their martyred blood and ashes sow
   O'er all th'Italian fields where still doth sway
The triple tyrant, that from these may grow
   A hundredfold, who having learnt thy way
   Early may fly the Babylonian woe.

JOHN MILTON

78 'When I consider how my light is spent'

WHEN I consider how my light is spent,
    Ere half my days, in this dark world and wide,
    And that one talent which is death to hide
    Lodged with me useless, though my soul more bent
To serve therewith my Maker, and present
    My true account, lest he returning chide,
    'Doth God exact day-labour, light denied?'
    I fondly ask. But patience to prevent
That murmur soon replies, 'God doth not need
    Either man's work or his own gifts; who best
    Bear his mild yoke, they serve him best, his state
Is kingly. Thousands at his bidding speed
    And post o'er land and ocean without rest:
    They also serve who only stand and wait.'

JOHN MILTON

79 'Methought I saw my late espousèd saint'

METHOUGHT I saw my late espousèd saint
    Brought to me like Alcestis from the grave,
    Whom Jove's great son to her glad husband gave,
    Rescued from death by force, though pale and faint.
Mine as whom washed from spot of child-bed taint,
    Purification in the old law did save,
    And such as yet once more I trust to have
    Full sight of her in heaven without restraint,
Came vested all in white, pure as her mind.
    Her face was veiled, yet to my fancied sight
    Love, sweetness, goodness in her person shined
So clear, as in no face with more delight.
    But oh as to embrace me she inclined,
    I waked, she fled, and day brought back my night.

JOHN MILTON

80–3 ### *Resolution in Four Sonnets, of a Poetical Question put to me by a Friend, concerning Four Rural Sisters*

❧ i ❧

ALICE is tall and upright as a pine,
White as blanched almonds or the falling snow,
Sweet as are damask roses when they blow,
And doubtless fruitful as the swelling vine.

Ripe to be cut, and ready to be pressed,
Her full-cheeked beauties very well appear,
And a year's fruit she loses every year,
Wanting a man t'improve her to the best.

Full fain she would be husbanded, and yet,
Alas! she cannot a fit lab'rer get
To cultivate her to her own content:

Fain would she be (God wot) about her task,
And yet (forsooth) she is too proud to ask,
And (which is worse) too modest to consent.

❀❀❀ ii ❀❀❀

MARGARET of humbler stature by the head
Is, as it oft falls out with yellow hair,
Than her fair sister yet so much more fair,
As her pure white is better mixed with red.

This, hotter than the other ten to one,
Longs to be put unto her mother's trade
And loud proclaims she lives too long a maid,
Wishing for one t'untie her virgin zone.

She finds virginity a kind of ware,
That's very very troublesome to bear,
And, being gone, she thinks will ne'er be missed:

And yet withal the girl has so much grace,
To call for help I know she wants the face,
Though asked, I know not how she would resist.

❧❧❧ iii ❧❧❧

MARY is black, and taller than the last,
Yet equal in perfection and desire
To the one's melting snow, and t'other's fire,
As with whose black their fairness is defaced.

She pants as much for love as th'other two,
But she so virtuous is, or else so wise,
That she will win or will not love a prize,
And but upon good terms will never do:

Therefore who will her conquer ought to be
At least as full of love and wit as she,
Or he shall ne'er gain favour at her hands:

Nay, though he have a pretty store of brains,
Shall only have his labour for his pains,
Unless he offer more than she demands.

❧❀❧ iv ❧❀❧

MARTHA is not so tall, nor yet so fair
As any of the other lovely three.
Her chiefest grace is poor simplicity,
Yet were the rest away, she were a star.

She's fair enough, only she wants the art
To set her beauties off as they can do,
And that's the cause she ne'er heard any woo.
Nor ever yet made conquest of a heart:

And yet her blood's as boiling as the best,
Which, pretty soul, does so disturb her rest,
And makes her languish so, she's fit to die.

Poor thing, I doubt she still must lie alone,
For being like to be attacked by none,
She's no more wit to ask than to deny.

CHARLES COTTON

84   *Cynthia on Horseback*

FAIR Cynthia mounted on her sprightly pad,
Which in white robe with silver fringe was clad,
    And swift as wind his graceful steps did move,
    As with his beauteous guide he'd been in love.

Though fierce, yet humble still to her command,
Obeying every touch of her fair hand;
    Her golden bit his foaming mouth did check,
    It spread his crest, and raised his bending neck.

She was the rose upon this hill of snow.
Her sparkling beauty made the glorious show
    Whence secret flames men in their bosoms took.
The graces and the cupids her surround,
Attending her, while cruel she does wound
    With switch her horse, and hearts with every look.

PHILIP AYRES

85 *Epitaph on the Tombstone of a Child,*
     the last of Seven that died before

THIS little, silent, gloomy monument
Contains all that was sweet and innocent,
The softest prattler that e'er found a tongue.
His voice was music and his words a song,
Which now each listening angel smiling hears,
Such pretty harmonies compose the spheres.
Wanton as unfledged cupids, ere their charms
Had learned the little arts of doing harms,
Fair as young cherubins, as soft and kind,
And though translated could not be refined,
The seventh dear pledge the nuptial joys had given,
Toiled here on earth, retired to rest in heaven,
Where they the shining host of angels fill,
Spread their gay wings before the throne, and smile.

APHRA BEHN

86 *On the Edition of Mr. Pope's Works*
with a Commentary and Notes

In evil hour did Pope's declining age,
  Deceived and dazzled by the tinsel show
  Of wordy science and the nauseous flow
Of mean officious flatteries, engage

Thy venal quill to deck his laboured page
  With ribald nonsense, and permit to strew,
  Amidst his flowers, the baleful weeds that grow
In th'unblessed soil of rude and rancorous rage.

Yet this the avenging Muse ordainèd so,
  When, by his counsel or weak sufferance,
    To thee were trusted Shakespeare's fame and fate.
She doom'd him down the stream of time to tow
  Thy foul, dirt-loaded hulk, or sink perchance,
    Dragged to oblivion by the foundering weight.

THOMAS EDWARDS

87   *On the Death of Richard West*

IN vain to me the smiling mornings shine,
And reddening Phoebus lifts his golden fire:
The birds in vain their amorous descant join,
Or cheerful fields resume their green attire:
These ears, alas! for other notes repine,
A different object do these eyes require.
My lonely anguish melts no heart but mine;
And in my breast the imperfect joys expire.
Yet morning smiles the busy race to cheer,
And new-born pleasure brings to happier men:
The fields to all their wonted tribute bear;
To warm their little loves the birds complain.
I fruitless mourn to him that cannot hear,
And weep the more because I weep in vain.

THOMAS GRAY

88 *On Bathing*

WHEN late the trees were stript by winter pale,
Young Health, a dryad-maid in vesture green,
Or like the forest's silver-quivered queen,
On airy uplands met the piercing gale;
And, ere its earliest echo shook the vale,
Watching the hunter's joyous horn was seen.
But since, gay-throned in fiery chariot sheen,
Summer has smote each daisy-dappled dale;
She to the cave retires, high-arched beneath
The fount that laves proud Isis' towery brim:
And now, all glad the temperate air to breathe,
While cooling drops distil from arches dim,
Binding her dewy locks with sedgy wreath,
She sits amid the quire of naiads trim.

THOMAS WARTON

89   *To the River Lodon*

AH! what a weary race my feet have run,
Since first I trod thy banks with alders crowned,
And thought my way was all through fairy ground,
Beneath thy azure sky, and golden sun:
Where first my Muse to lisp her notes begun!
While pensive memory traces back the round,
Which fills the varied interval between;
Much pleasure, more of sorrow, marks the scene.
Sweet native stream! those skies and suns so pure
No more return, to cheer my evening road!
Yet still one joy remains, that not obscure,
Nor useless, all my vacant days have flowed,
From youth's grey dawn to manhood's prime mature;
Nor with the Muse's laurel unbestowed.

THOMAS WARTON

90   *To George Romney, esq.*

On his picture of me in crayons, drawn at Eartham
in the sixty-first year of my age, and in the months of
August and September, 1792

❧❧❧

ROMNEY! expert infallibly to trace,
On chart or canvas, not the form alone,
And semblance, but, however faintly shown,
The mind's impression too on ev'ry face,
With strokes that time ought never to erase:
Thou hast so penciled mine, that though I own
The subject worthless, I have never known
The artist shining with superior grace.
But this I mark, that symptoms none of woe
In thy incomparable work appear:
Well! I am satisfied it should be so,
Since, on maturer thought, the cause is clear;
      For in my looks what sorrow could'st thou see
      When I was Hayley's guest, and sat to thee?

WILLIAM COWPER

92

91   *To the Poppy*

WHILE summer roses all their glory yield
  To crown the votary of Love and Joy,
  Misfortune's victim hails, with many a sigh,
  Thee, scarlet poppy of the pathless field,
Gaudy, yet wild and lone; no leaf to shield
  Thy flaccid vest, that, as the gale blows high,
  Flaps, and alternate folds around thy head. —
  So stands in the long grass a love-crazed maid
Smiling aghast; while stream to every wind
  Her garish ribbons, smeared with dust and rain;
  But brain-sick visions cheat her tortured mind,
And bring false peace. Thus, lulling grief and pain,
  Kind dreams oblivious from thy juice proceed,
  Thou flimsy, showy, melancholy weed.

ANNA SEWARD

92 *To a Nightingale*

Poor melancholy bird—that all night long
   Tell'st to the moon thy tale of tender woe;
   From what sad cause can such sweet sorrow flow,
And whence this mournful melody of song?

Thy poet's musing fancy would translate
   What mean the sounds that swell thy little breast,
   When still at dewy eve thou leav'st thy nest,
Thus to the listening night to sing thy fate?

Pale Sorrow's victims wert thou once among,
   Tho' now released in woodlands wild to rove?
   Say—hast thou felt from friends some cruel wrong,
Or died'st thou—martyr of disastrous love?
Ah! songstress sad! that such my lot might be,
To sigh and sing at liberty—like thee!

CHARLOTTE SMITH

93 *Composed during a Walk on the Downs,
in November 1787*

THE dark and pillowy cloud; the sallow trees,
Seem o'er the ruins of the year to mourn;
And cold and hollow, the inconstant breeze
Sobs thro' the falling leaves and withered fern.
O'er the tall brow of yonder chalky bourn,
The evening-shades their gathered darkness fling,
While, by the lingering light, I scare discern
The shrieking night-jar, sail on heavy wing.
Ah! yet a little—and propitious Spring
Crowned with fresh flowers, shall wake the woodland strain;
But no gay change revolving seasons bring,
To call forth pleasure from the soul of pain,
Bid syren Hope resume her long-lost part,
And chase the vulture Care—that feeds upon the heart.

CHARLOTTE SMITH

94 *To Fancy*

THEE, queen of shadows!—shall I still invoke,
Still love the scenes thy sportive pencil drew,
When on mine eyes the early radience broke
Which shew'd the beauteous, rather than the true!
Alas! long since, those glowing tints are dead,
And now 'tis thine in darkest hues to dress
The spot where pale Experience hangs her head
O'er the sad grave of murdered Happiness!
Thro' thy false medium then, no longer viewed,
May fancied pain and fancied pleasure fly,
And I, as from me all thy dreams depart,
Be to my wayward destiny subdued;
Nor seek perfection with a poet's eye,
Nor suffer anguish with a poet's heart!

CHARLOTTE SMITH

95 *To the Insect of the Gossamer*

SMALL, viewless æronaut, that by the line
    Of gossamer suspended, in mid air
    Float'st on a sun beam—living atom, where
Ends thy breeze-guided voyage;—with what design
    In æther dost thou launch thy form minute,
Mocking the eye?—Alas! before the veil
    Of denser clouds shall hide thee, the pursuit
Of the keen swift may end thy fairy sail!—
    Thus on the golden thread that Fancy weaves
Buoyant, as Hope's illusive flattery breathes,
    The young and visionary poet leaves
Life's dull realities, while sevenfold wreaths
    Of rainbow-light around his head revolve.
    Ah! soon at Sorrow's touch the radiant dreams dissolve!

CHARLOTTE SMITH

96   *On a Wet Summer*

ALL ye who far from town in rural hall,
    Like me, were wont to dwell near pleasant field,
    Enjoying all the sunny day did yield,
    With me the change lament, in irksome thrall,
By rains incessant held; for now no call
    From early swain invites my hand to wield
    The scythe; in parlour dim I sit concealed,
    And mark the lessening sand from hour-glass fall,
Or 'neath my window view the wistful train
    Of dripping poultry, whom the vine's broad leaves
    Shelter no more.—Mute is the mournful plain,
Silent the swallow sits beneath the thatch,
    And vacant hind hangs pensive o'er his hatch,
    Counting the frequent drop from reeded eaves.

JOHN BAMPFYLDE

97 *To Liberty*

OH! Liberty! transcendent and sublime!
  Born on the mountain's solitary crest;
Nature thy nurse, thy sire unconquered time,
  Truth, the pure inmate of thy glowing breast!
Oft dost thou wander by the billowy deep,
  Scattering the sands that bind the level shore,
Or, towering, brave the desolating roar
  That bids the tyrant tempest lash the steep!
'Tis thine, when sanguinary daemons lour,
  Amidst the thickening hosts to force thy way;
To quell the minions of oppressive power,
  And shame the vaunting nothings of a day!
Still shall the human mind thy name adore,
  Till chaos reigns—and worlds shall be no more!

MARY ROBINSON

98   *To the River Itchin, near Winton*

ITCHIN, where I behold thy banks again,
   Thy crumbling margin, and thy silver breast,
   On which the self-same tints still seem to rest,
Why feels my heart the shiv'ring sense of pain?
   Is it, that many a summer's day has past
Since, in life's morn, I caroled on thy side?
Is it, that oft, since then, my heart has sighed,
   As Youth, and Hope's delusive gleams, flew fast?
Is it that those, who circled on thy shore,
Companions of my youth, now meet no more?
   Whate'er the cause, upon thy banks I bend
Sorrowing, yet feel such solace at my heart,
   As at the meeting of some long-lost friend,
   From whom, in happier hours, we wept to part.

WILLIAM LISLE BOWLES

99 *On the Death of William Linley, esq.,*
The composer of the music of 'The Duenna,' etc.

POOR Linley! I shall miss thee sadly, now
Thou art not in the world; for few remain
Who loved like thee the high and holy strain
Of harmony's immortal master.
                                    Thou
Didst honour him; and none I know, who live,
Could even a shadow, a faint image give,
With chord and voice, of those rich harmonies,
Which, mingled in one mighty volume, rise,
Glorious, from earth to heaven, so to express
Choral acclaim to Heaven's almightiness,
As thou! Therefore, amid the world's deep roar,
When the sweet visions of young Hope are fled,
And many friends dispersed, and many dead,
I grieve that I shall hear that voice no more.

WILLIAM LISLE BOWLES

100

To Hope

OH, ever skilled to wear the form we love!
To bid the shapes of fear and grief depart,
Come, gentle Hope! with one gay smile remove
The lasting sadness of an aching heart.
Thy voice, benign enchantress! let me hear;
Say that for me some pleasures yet shall bloom!
That fancy's radiance, friendship's precious tear
Shall soften, or shall chase, misfortune's gloom.—
But come not glowing in the dazzling ray
Which once with dear illusions charmed my eye!
Oh strew no more, sweet flatterer! on my way
The flowers I fondly thought too bright to die.
Visions less fair will sooth my pensive breast,
That asks not happiness, but longs for rest!

HELEN MARIA WILLIAMS

101 *To the Strawberry*

THE strawberry blooms upon its lowly bed,
Plant of my native soil!—the lime may fling
More potent fragrance on the zephyr's wing;
The milky cocoa richer juices shed;
The white guava lovelier blossoms spread—
But not like thee to fond remembrance bring
The vanished hours of life's enchanting spring,
Short calendar of joys for ever fled!—
Thou bidst the scenes of childhood rise to view,
The wild-wood path which fancy loves to trace;
Where veiled in leaves, thy fruit of rosy hue
Lurked on its pliant stem with modest grace—
But ah! when thought would later years renew,
Alas, successive sorrows crowd the space!

HELEN MARIA WILLIAMS

102 *To Boccaccio*

Not for thy gothic trumpet's martial rage,
   Not for thy Latin bays, nor that 'twas thine
   The Tuscan's rugged period to refine,
   Nor yet, Boccaccio, that thy faithful page
Reflects the genuine manners of thy age,
   Nor that, enlivened at thy sprightlier style,
   Pale Sorrow's victims smooth the brow, and smile;
   For nought of worth like this, immortal sage,
Haste I to twine this garland round thy tomb;
   But that I oft have shar'd Nastagio's fears
   At his dread vision, oft have wept the doom
Of fair Ghismonda, sunk in early years,
   I crown thee with this chaplet's simple bloom,
   The bard sublime of terror, and of tears.

THOMAS RUSSELL

103   *Composed upon Westminster Bridge,*
      September 3, 1802

EARTH has not anything to show more fair;
Dull would he be of soul who could pass by
A sight so touching in its majesty:
This city now doth, like a garment, wear
The beauty of the morning; silent, bare,
Ships, towers, domes, theatres, and temples lie
Open unto the fields, and to the sky;
All bright and glittering in the smokeless air.
Never did sun more beautifully steep
In his first splendour, valley, rock, or hill;
Ne'er saw I, never felt, a calm so deep!
The river glideth at his own sweet will:
Dear God! the very houses seem asleep;
And all that mighty heart is lying still!

WILLIAM WORDSWORTH

September 1, 1802

104

Among the capricious acts of tyranny that disgraced
those times, was the chasing of all Negroes from France
by decree of the government: we had a fellow-passenger
who was one of the expelled.

WE had a female passenger who came
From Calais with us, spotless in array,—
A white-robed Negro, like a lady gay,
Yet downcast as a woman fearing blame;
Meek, destitute, as seemed, of hope or aim
She sate, from notice turning not away,
But on all proffered intercourse did lay
A weight of languid speech, or to the same
No sign of answer made by word or face:
Yet still her eyes retained their tropic fire,
That, burning independent of the mind,
Joined with the lustre of her rich attire
To mock the outcast—O ye Heavens, be kind!
And feel, thou Earth, for this afflicted race!

WILLIAM WORDSWORTH

105   *'Surprised by joy—impatient as the wind'*

❧❧❧

SURPRISED by joy—impatient as the wind
I turned to share the transport—Oh! with whom
But thee, deep buried in the silent tomb,
That spot which no vicissitude can find?
Love, faithful love, recalled thee to my mind—
But how could I forget thee? Through what power,
Even for the least division of an hour,
Have I been so beguiled as to be blind
To my most grievous loss!—That thought's return
Was the worst pang that sorrow ever bore,
Save one, one only, when I stood forlorn,
Knowing my heart's best treasure was no more;
That neither present time, nor years unborn
Could to my sight that heavenly face restore.

WILLIAM WORDSWORTH

106 *The Faery Chasm*

No fiction was it of the antique age:
A sky-blue stone, within this sunless cleft,
Is of the very footmarks unbereft
Which tiny elves impressed;—on that smooth stage
Dancing with all their brilliant equipage
In secret revels—haply after theft
Of some sweet babe—flower stolen, and coarse weed left
For the distracted mother to assuage
Her grief with, as she might!—But, where, oh! where
Is traceable a vestige of the notes
That ruled those dances wild in character?—
Deep underground? Or in the upper air,
On the shrill wind of midnight? or where floats
O'er twilight fields the autumnal gossamer?

WILLIAM WORDSWORTH

107   *'I watch, and long have watched,*
with calm regret'

I WATCH, and long have watched, with calm regret
Yon slowly-sinking star—immortal sire
(So might he seem) of all the glittering quire!
Blue ether still surrounds him—yet—and yet;
But now the horizon's rocky parapet
Is reached, where, forfeiting his bright attire,
He burns—transmuted to a dusky fire—
Then pays submissively the appointed debt
To the flying moments, and is seen no more.
Angels and gods! We struggle with our fate,
While health, power, glory, from their height decline,
Depressed; and then extinguished: and our state,
In this, how different, lost star, from thine,
That no to-morrow shall our beams restore!

WILLIAM WORDSWORTH

108   *The Column intended by Buonaparte*
for a triumphal edifice in Milan, now
lying by the way-side in the Simplon Pass

AMBITION—following down this far-famed slope
Her pioneer, the snow-dissolving sun,
While clarions prate of kingdoms to be won—
Perchance, in future ages, here may stop;
Taught to mistrust her flattering horoscope
By admonition from this prostrate stone!
Memento uninscribed of Pride o'erthrown;
Vanity's hieroglyphic; a choice trope
In Fortune's rhetoric. Daughter of the rock,
Rest where thy course was stayed by power divine!
The soul transported sees, from hint of thine,
Crimes which the great avenger's hand provoke,
Hears combats whistling o'er the ensanguined heath:
What groans! what shrieks! what quietness in death!

WILLIAM WORDSWORTH

109   *'Scorn not the sonnet;*
         critic, you have frowned'

SCORN not the sonnet; critic, you have frowned,
Mindless of its just honours; with this key
Shakespeare unlocked his heart; the melody
Of this small lute gave ease to Petrarch's wound;
A thousand times this pipe did Tasso sound;
With it Camöens soothed an exile's grief;
The sonnet glittered a gay myrtle leaf
Amid the cypress with which Dante crowned
His visionary brow: a glow-worm lamp,
It cheered mild Spenser, called from Faery-land
To struggle through the dark ways; and, when a damp
Fell round the path of Milton, in his hand
The thing became a trumpet; whence he blew
Soul-animating strains—alas, too few!

WILLIAM WORDSWORTH

110   *A Tradition of Oker Hill in*
        Darley Dale, Derbyshire

'TIS said that to the brow of yon fair hill
Two brothers clomb, and, turning face from face,
Nor one look more exchanging, grief to still
Or feed, each planted on that lofty place
A chosen tree; then, eager to fulfil
Their courses, like two new-born rivers, they
In opposite directions urged their way
Down from the far-seen mount. No blast might kill
Or blight that fond memorial;—the trees grew,
And now entwine their arms; but ne'er again
Embraced those brothers upon earth's wide plain;
Nor aught of mutual joy or sorrow knew
Until their spirits mingled in the sea
That to itself takes all, Eternity.

WILLIAM WORDSWORTH

111 *To the River Otter*

Dear native brook! wild streamlet of the west!
  How many various-fated years have past,
  What happy and what mournful hours, since last
I skimmed the smooth thin stone along thy breast,
Numbering its light leaps! yet so deep imprest
Sink the sweet scenes of childhood, that mine eyes
  I never shut amid the sunny ray,
But straight with all their tints thy waters rise,
  Thy crossing plank, thy marge with willows grey,
And bedded sand that veined with various dyes
Gleamed through thy bright transparence! On my way,
  Visions of childhood! oft have ye beguiled
Lone manhood's cares, yet waking fondest sighs:
  Ah! that once more I were a careless child!

SAMUEL TAYLOR COLERIDGE

112 *Koskiusko*

O H what a loud and fearful shriek was there,
  As though a thousand souls one death-groan poured!
  Ah me! they saw beneath a hireling's sword
Their Koskiusko fall! Through the swart air
(As pauses the tired cossack's barbarous yell
  Of triumph) on the chill and midnight gale
  Rises with frantic burst or sadder swell
The dirge of murdered Hope! while Freedom pale
Bends in such anguish o'er her destined bier,
  As if from eldest time some spirit meek
  Had gathered in a mystic urn each tear
That ever on a patriot's furrowed cheek
Fit channel found; and she had drained the bowl
In the mere wilfulness, and sick despair of soul!

December 16, 1794

SAMUEL TAYLOR COLERIDGE

113 *Composed on a journey homeward;
the author having received intelligence of
the birth of a son, Sept. 20, 1796*

O FT o'er my brain does that strange fancy roll
   Which makes the present (while the flash doth last)
   Seem a mere semblance of some unknown past,
Mixed with such feelings, as perplex the soul
Self-questioned in her sleep; and some have said
   We lived, ere yet this robe of flesh we wore.
   O my sweet baby! when I reach my door,
If heavy looks should tell me thou art dead,
(As sometimes, through excess of hope, I fear)
I think that I should struggle to believe
   Thou wert a spirit, to this nether sphere
Sentenced for some more venial crime to grieve;
Did'st scream, then spring to meet Heaven's quick reprieve,
   While we wept idly o'er thy little bier!

SAMUEL TAYLOR COLERIDGE

114 *To Nature*

I T may indeed be fantasy, when I
   Essay to draw from all created things
   Deep, heartfelt, inward joy that closely clings;
And trace in leaves and flowers that round me lie
Lessons of love and earnest piety.
   So let it be; and if the wide world rings
   In mock of this belief, it brings
Nor fear, nor grief, nor vain perplexity.
So will I build my altar in the fields,
   And the blue sky my fretted dome shall be,
And the sweet fragrance that the wild flower yields
   Shall be the incense I will yield to Thee,
Thee only God! and thou shalt not despise
Even me, the priest of this poor sacrifice.

SAMUEL TAYLOR COLERIDGE

115 *Work without Hope*

Lines composed 21st February 1825

❧❧❧

ALL nature seems at work. Slugs leave their lair—
The bees are stirring—birds are on the wing—
And Winter slumbering in the open air,
Wears on his smiling face a dream of Spring!
And I the while, the sole unbusy thing,
Nor honey make, nor pair, nor build, nor sing.

Yet well I ken the banks where amaranths blow,
Have traced the fount whence streams of nectar flow.
Bloom, O ye amaranths! bloom for whom ye may,
For me ye bloom not! Glide, rich streams, away!
With lips unbrightened, wreathless brow, I stroll:
And would you learn the spells that drowse my soul?
Work without hope draws nectar in a sieve,
And hope without an object cannot live.

SAMUEL TAYLOR COLERIDGE

116   *Written in Autumn*

O AUTUMN! how I love thy pensive air,
   Thy yellow garb, thy visage sad and dun!
   When from the misty east the labouring sun
Bursts through thy fogs, that gathering round him, dare
Obscure his beams, which, though enfeebled, dart
   On the cold, dewy plains a lustre bright:
   But chief, the sound of thy reft woods delight;
Their deep, low murmurs to my soul impart
A solemn stillness, while they seem to speak
   Of Spring, of Summer now for ever past,
   Of drear, approaching Winter, and the blast
Which shall ere long their soothing quiet break:
   Here, when for faded joys my heaving breast
   Throbs with vain pangs, here will I love to rest.

MARY TIGHE

117   *Written at the Eagle's Nest,*

Killarney

JULY 26, 1800

❦❦❦

HERE let us rest, while with meridan blaze
    The sun rides glorious 'mid the cloudless sky,
    While o'er the lake no cooling zephyrs fly,
But on the liquid glass we dazzled gaze,
And fainting ask for shade: lo! where his nest
    The bird of Jove has fixed: the lofty brow,
With arbutus and fragrant wild shrubs drest,
    Impendent frowns, nor will approach allow:
Here the soft turf invites; here magic sounds
    Celestially respondent shall enchant,
While melody from yon steep wood rebounds
    In thrilling cadence sweet. Sure, life can grant
No brighter hours than this; and memory oft
Shall paint this happiest scene with pencil soft.

MARY TIGHE

118 *'A wrinkled crabbèd man they picture thee'*

A WRINKLED crabbèd man they picture thee,
Old Winter, with a ragged beard as grey
As the long moss upon the apple-tree;
Close muffled up, and on thy dreary way,
Blue lipt, an ice drop at thy sharp blue nose,
Plodding alone through sleet and drifting snows.
They should have drawn thee by the high-heapt hearth,
Old Winter! seated in thy great armed chair,
Watching the children at their Christmas mirth
Or circled by them as their lips declare
Some merry jest or tale of murder dire,
Or troubled spirit that disturbs the night,
Pausing at times to move the languid fire,
Or taste the old October brown and bright.

ROBERT SOUTHEY

119 *The Gipsy's Malison*

'SUCK, baby, suck, mother's love grows by giving,
Drain the sweet founts that only thrive by wasting;
Black manhood comes, when riotous guilty living
Hands thee the cup that shall be death in tasting.

Kiss, baby, kiss, mother's lips shine by kisses,
Choke the warm breath that else would fall in blessings;
Black manhood comes, when turbulent guilty blisses
Tend thee the kiss that poisons 'mid caressings.

Hang, baby, hang, mother's love loves such forces,
Strain the fond neck that bends still to thy clinging;
Black manhood comes, when violent lawless courses
Leave thee a spectacle in rude air swinging.'

So sang a withered beldam energetical,
And banned the ungiving door with lips prophetical.

CHARLES LAMB

120

To Dora W[ordsworth],

On Being Asked by Her Father to Write in Her Album

AN album is a banquet: from the store,
In his intelligential orchard growing,
Your sire might heap your board to overflowing;—
One shaking of the tree—'twould ask no more
To set a salad forth, more rich than that
Which Evelyn in his princely cookery fancied:
Or that more rare, by Eve's neat hands enhancèd,
Where, a pleased guest, the angelic Virtue sat.
But like the all-grasping founder of the feast,
Whom Nathan to the sinning king did tax,
From his less wealthy neighbours he exacts;
Spares his own flocks, and takes the poor man's beast.
Obedient to his bidding, lo, I am,
A zealous, meek, *contributory*

LAMB.

121   *To Arthur de Noé Walker*

ARTHUR! whose path is in the quiet shade,
After hot days in the wide wastes of war,
Where India saw thy sword shine bright above
The helms of thousand brave. Peace, wooed and won,
Could not detain thee from that Tauric coast
Where lay the wounded, festering in their gore,
And none to raise them up, thou hastenedst
To succour: often thy strong shoulder bore
Amid the fiery sleet and heavier hail
The wretch whom Death looked down on and past by:
Thou fearèdst not, for what hadst thou to fear
From Death? the standard of his vanquisher
Thou never hast deserted; thee he called
To work his will, and saw the call obeyed.

WALTER SAVAGE LANDOR

122 *The Fatal Birth*

FOUL parent of fair child, swoll'n Breadtax! thou
On plundered commerce didst beget Reform:
We see a bright tomorrow on her brow,
And make our hope thy nursling of the storm.
But many a fanged worm and biped brute,
On whose dark heart the eye of love ne'er smiled,
Would fain the promise of her morn refute.
Die then, dread power! and have no other child;
For it is written, that thy second-born,
If second-born thou have, will thunder-strike
Temple and tower, of strength and splendour shorn
By hands with famine lean; and, Samson-like,
Shaking the pillars of the gold-roofed state,
Whelm high, and low, and all, in one remorseless fate.

EBENEZER ELLIOTT

123   *To the Grasshopper and the Cricket*

GREEN little vaulter in the sunny grass,
   Catching your heart up at the feel of June,
   Sole voice that's heard amidst the lazy noon,
When ev'n the bees lag at the summoning brass;—
And you, warm little housekeeper, who class
   With those who think the candles come too soon,
   Loving the fire, and with your tricksome tune
Nick the glad silent moments as they pass;—

Oh sweet and tiny cousins, that belong,
   One to the fields, the other to the hearth,
Both have your sunshine; both, though small, are strong
   At your clear hearts; and both were sent on earth
To sing in thoughtful ears this natural song—
   In doors and out,—summer and winter,—mirth.

JAMES HENRY LEIGH HUNT

124–6   *The Fish, the Man, and the Spirit*

TO A FISH

You strange, astonished-looking, angle-faced,
   Dreary-mouthed, gaping wretches of the sea,
   Gulping salt-water everlastingly,
Cold-blooded, though with red your blood be graced,
And mute, though dwellers in the roaring waste;
   And you, all shapes beside, that fishy be,—
   Some round, some flat, some long, all devilry,
Legless, unloving, infamously chaste:—

O scaly, slippery, wet, swift, staring wights,
   What is't ye do? What life lead? eh, dull goggles?
How do ye vary your vile days and nights?
   How pass your Sundays? Are ye still but joggles
In ceaseless wash? Still nought but gapes, and bites,
   And drinks, and stares, diversified with boggles?

A FISH ANSWERS

AMAZING monster! that, for aught I know,
    With the first sight of thee didst make our race
    For ever stare! O flat and shocking face,
Grimly divided from the breast below!
Thou that on dry land horribly dost go
    With a split body and most ridiculous pace,
    Prong after prong, disgracer of all grace,
Long-useless-finned, haired, upright, unwet, slow!
O breather of unbreathable, sword-sharp air,
    How canst exist? How bear thyself, thou dry
And dreary sloth? What particle canst share
    Of the only blessèd life, the watery?
I sometimes see of ye an actual *pair*
    Go by! linked fin by fin! most odiously.

❧❧ ❧❧

THE FISH TURNS INTO A MAN, AND THEN INTO A SPIRIT, AND AGAIN SPEAKS

INDULGE thy smiling scorn, if smiling still,
　　O man! and loathe, but with a sort of love:
　　For difference must its use by difference prove,
And, in sweet clang, the spheres with music fill.
One of the spirits am I, that at his will
　　Live in whate'er has life—fish, eagle, dove—
　　No hate, nor pride, beneath nought, nor above,
A visitor of the rounds of God's sweet skill.

Man's life is warm, glad, sad, 'twixt loves and graves,
　　Boundless in hope, honoured with pangs austere,
Heaven-gazing; and his angel-wings he craves:—
　　The fish is swift, small-needing, vague yet clear,
A cold, sweet, silver life, wrapped in round waves,
　　Quickened with touches of transporting fear.

JAMES HENRY LEIGH HUNT

127   *Iterating Sonnet*

Written during the talk of a war between
England and the United States

❦❦❦

WAR between England and the United States!
   Impossible! Pshaw! Stuff!—'United States!'
   Why, they themselves are the United States:
   London and Boston are United States:
New York and Liverpool United States:
   Cotton and spinning very United States:
   Progress and liberty, United States:
   Their names, fames, books, bloods, all United States.
But 'bloods are up' in the United States?
   Well;—would'st have 'low' bloods in the United States?
   No: high bloods—high—in both United States:
So high, that, seeing their United States,
   They scorn to stoop from such United States
   Solely to please poor *dis*-United States.

JAMES HENRY LEIGH HUNT

128 *To Genevra*

THY cheek is pale with thought, but not from woe,
  And yet so lovely, that if mirth could flush
  Its rose of whiteness with the brightest blush,
My heart would wish away that ruder glow:—
And dazzle not thy deep-blue eyes—but, oh!
  While gazing on them sterner eyes will gush,
  And into mine my mother's weakness rush,
Soft as the last drops round heaven's airy bow.
For, through thy long dark lashes low depending,
  The soul of melancholy gentleness
Gleams like a seraph from the sky descending,
  Above all pain, yet pitying all distress;
At once such majesty with sweetness blending,
  I worship more, but cannot love thee less.

GEORGE GORDON, LORD BYRON

129 *Malvern at a Distance*

SOFT ridge of cloud or mountain! which thou art
   I know not well; so delicately fine
   Swells to mine eye the undulating line,
Where gazing to and fro, as loth to part,
Unwearied Fancy plies her busy part,
   To trace what lurks in those deep folds of thine,
   Streaked by the varying heavens with hues divine.
With me 'tis fancy all; but many a heart
   Perchance e'en now perusing thee afar
   The meaning reads of every spot and wave
   That seems to stain thee, or thine outline mar.
Here is their home, and here their father's grave.
   Such is our holy Mount; all dream it fair,
Those only know, whom Faith hath nurtured there.

JOHN KEBLE

130   *England in 1819*

An old, mad, blind, despised, and dying king,—
Princes, the dregs of their dull race, who flow
Through public scorn,—mud from a muddy spring,—
Rulers who neither see, nor feel, nor know,
But leech-like to their fainting country cling,
Till they drop, blind in blood, without a blow,—
A people starved and stabbed in the untilled field,—
An army, which liberticide and prey
Makes as a two-edged sword to all who wield,—
Golden and sanguine laws which tempt and slay;
Religion Christless, Godless—a book sealed;
A Senate,—Time's worst statute unrepealed,—
Are graves, from which a glorious phantom may
Burst, to illumine our tempestuous day.

PERCY BYSSHE SHELLEY

131–5 *Ode to the West Wind*

i

O WILD West Wind, thou breath of Autumn's being,
Thou, from whose unseen presence the leaves dead
Are driven, like ghosts from an enchanter fleeing,

Yellow, and black, and pale, and hectic red,
Pestilence-stricken multitudes: O thou,
Who chariotest to their dark wintry bed

The wingèd seeds, where they lie cold and low,
Each like a corpse within its grave, until
Thine azure sister of the Spring shall blow

Her clarion o'er the dreaming earth, and fill
(Driving sweet buds like flocks to feed in air)
With living hues and odours plain and hill:

Wild Spirit, which art moving everywhere;
Destroyer and preserver; hear, oh, hear!

❧❧❧ ii ❧❧❧

THOU on whose stream, mid the steep sky's commotion,
Loose clouds like earth's decaying leaves are shed,
Shook from the tangled boughs of Heaven and Ocean,

Angels of rain and lightning: there are spread
On the blue surface of thine aëry surge,
Like the bright hair uplifted from the head

Of some fierce maenad, even from the dim verge
Of the horizon to the zenith's height,
The locks of the approaching storm. Thou dirge

Of the dying year, to which this closing night
Will be the dome of a vast sepulchre,
Vaulted with all thy congregated might

Of vapours, from whose solid atmosphere
Black rain, and fire, and hail will burst: oh, hear!

❀❀❀ iii ❀❀❀

THOU who didst waken from his summer dreams
The blue Mediterranean, where he lay,
Lulled by the coil of his crystàlline streams,

Beside a pumice isle in Baiae's bay,
And saw in sleep old palaces and towers
Quivering within the wave's intenser day,

All overgrown with azure moss and flowers
So sweet, the sense faints picturing them! Thou
For whose path the Atlantic's level powers

Cleave themselves into chasms, while far below
The sea-blooms and the oozy woods which wear
The sapless foliage of the ocean, know

Thy voice, and suddenly grow gray with fear,
And tremble and despoil themselves: oh, hear!

❧❧❧ iv ❧❧❧

IF I were a dead leaf thou mightest bear;
If I were a swift cloud to fly with thee;
A wave to pant beneath thy power, and share

The impulse of thy strength, only less free
Than thou, O uncontrollable! If even
I were as in my boyhood, and could be

The comrade of thy wanderings over Heaven,
As then, when to outstrip thy skiey speed
Scarce seemed a vision; I would ne'er have striven

As thus with thee in prayer in my sore need.
Oh, lift me as a wave, a leaf, a cloud!
I fall upon the thorns of life! I bleed!

A heavy weight of hours has chained and bowed
One too like thee: tameless, and swift, and proud.

V

MAKE me thy lyre, even as the forest is:
What if my leaves are falling like its own!
The tumult of thy mighty harmonies

Will take from both a deep, autumnal tone,
Sweet though in sadness. Be thou, Spirit fierce,
My spirit! Be thou me, impetuous one!

Drive my dead thoughts over the universe
Like withered leaves to quicken a new birth!
And, by the incantation of this verse,

Scatter, as from an unextinguished hearth
Ashes and sparks, my words among mankind!
Be through my lips to unawakened earth

The trumpet of a prophecy! Oh, Wind,
If Winter comes, can Spring be far behind?

PERCY BYSSHE SHELLEY

136   *Ozymandias*

I MET a traveller from an antique land
Who said: Two vast and trunkless legs of stone
Stand in the desert . . . Near them, on the sand,
Half sunk, a shattered visage lies, whose frown,
And wrinkled lip, and sneer of cold command,
Tell that its sculptor well those passions read
Which yet survive, stamped on these lifeless things,
The hand that mocked them, and the heart that fed:
And on the pedestal these words appear:
'My name is Ozymandias, king of kings:
Look on my works, ye mighty, and despair!'
Nothing beside remains. Round the decay
Of that colossal wreck, boundless and bare
The lone and level sands stretch far away.

PERCY BYSSHE SHELLEY

137   *The Ants*

WHAT wonder strikes the curious while he views
The black ants' city by a rotten tree
Or woodland bank. In ignorance we muse,
Pausing amazed. We know not what we see,
Such government and order there to be:
Some looking on and urging some to toil,
Dragging their loads of bent stalks slavishly.
And what's more wonderful, big loads that foil
One ant or two to carry quickly; then
A swarm flocks round to help their fellow men.
Surely they speak a language whisperingly,
Too fine for us to hear, and sure their ways
Prove they have kings and laws, and them to be
Deformèd remnants of the fairy days.

JOHN CLARE

138 ## *'I am'*

I FEEL I am;—I only know I am,
And plod upon the earth, as dull and void:
Earth's prison chilled my body with its dram
Of dullness, and my soaring thoughts destroyed,
I fled to solitudes from passion's dream,
But strife pursued—I only know, I am,
I was a being created in the race
Of men disdaining bounds of place and time:—
A spirit that could travel o'er the space
Of earth and heaven,—like a thought sublime,
Tracing creation, like my maker, free,—
A soul unshackled—like eternity,
Spurning earth's vain and soul debasing thrall
But now I only know I am,—that's all.

JOHN CLARE

139 *The Maple Tree*

THE maple with its tassel flowers of green
That turns to red, a stag-horn shapèd seed
Just spreading out its scalloped leaves is seen,
Of yellowish hue yet beautifully green,
Bark ribbed like corduroy in seamy screed
That farther up the stem is smoother seen,
Where the white hemlock, with white umbel, flowers
Up each spread stoven to the branches' towers
And, mossy round the stoven, spread dark green
And blocked-leaved orchis and the bluebell flowers.
Thickly they grow and 'neath the leaves are seen.
I love to see them gemmed with morning hours;
I love the lone green places where they be
And the sweet clothing of the maple tree.

JOHN CLARE

140 *The Free-booter*

As the prey-freighted eagle cleaves the storm
With potent wing; while, at his scream and clang
To warn his famished brood, the hollow hills
Reverberate far and near; beneath his flight
The valley darkens, and his cloudy form
Swims up the sward to meet him as he glides
Into his mountain-nest: so comes Manrique
The single fear of many a province round.
Robber and outlaw!—A mere jot of life
Midst the still-standing rocks and precipices,
He moves right upward to his craggy dome
Scooped in the pinnacle. His horn, by times,
Shrill-throated, splits its voice among the rocks,
And sooty visages look out and smile!

GEORGE DARLEY

141   *On First Looking into Chapman's Homer*

MUCH have I travelled in the realms of gold,
　　And many goodly states and kingdoms seen;
　　Round many western islands have I been
Which bards in fealty to Apollo hold.
Oft of one wide expanse had I been told
　　That deep-browed Homer ruled as his demesne;
　　Yet did I never breathe its pure serene
Till I heard Chapman speak out loud and bold.

Then felt I like some watcher of the skies
　　When a new planet swims into his ken;
Or like stout Cortez when with eagle eyes
　　He stared at the Pacific, and all his men
Looked at each other with a wild surmise—
　　Silent, upon a peak in Darien.

JOHN KEATS

142 *To Mrs. Reynolds's Cat*

CAT, who hast passed thy grand climacteric,
   How many mice and rats hast in thy days
   Destroyed? How many titbits stolen? Gaze
With those bright languid segments green, and prick
Those velvet ears—but prithee do not stick
   Thy latent talons in me, and upraise
   Thy gentle mew, and tell me all thy frays
Of fish and mice, and rats and tender chick.
Nay, look not down, nor lick thy dainty wrists—
   For all the wheezy asthma, and for all
Thy tail's tip is nicked off, and though the fists
   Of many a maid have given thee many a maul,
Still is that fur as soft as when the lists
   In youth thou enteredst on glass-bottled wall.

JOHN KEATS

143   *'Blue! 'Tis the life of heaven, the domain'*

BLUE! 'Tis the life of heaven, the domain
    Of Cynthia, the wide palace of the sun,
The tent of Hesperus and all his train,
    The bosomer of clouds, gold, grey and dun.
Blue! 'Tis the life of waters. Ocean
    And all its vassal streams, pools numberless,
May rage, and foam, and fret, but never can
    Subside, if not to dark blue nativeness.
Blue! Gentle cousin of the forest-green,
    Married to green in all the sweetest flowers—
Forget-me-not, the blue bell, and that queen
    Of secrecy, the violet! What strange powers
Hast thou as a mere shadow! But how great,
When in an eye thou art alive with fate!

JOHN KEATS

144   *To Sleep*

O SOFT embalmer of the still midnight,
    Shutting with careful fingers and benign
Our gloom-pleased eyes, embowered from the light,
    Enshaded in forgetfulness divine:
O soothest Sleep! If so it please thee, close,
    In midst of this thine hymn, my willing eyes,
Or wait the 'Amen', ere thy poppy throws
    Around my bed its lulling charities.
Then save me, or the passèd day will shine
Upon my pillow, breeding many woes;
    Save me from curious conscience, that still hoards
Its strength for darkness, burrowing like a mole;
    Turn the key deftly in the oilèd wards,
And seal the hushèd casket of my soul.

JOHN KEATS

145 *'Bright star! Would I were steadfast
as thou art'*

BRIGHT star! Would I were steadfast as thou art—
   Not in lone splendour hung aloft the night
And watching, with eternal lids apart,
   Like nature's patient, sleepless eremite,
The moving waters at their priestlike task
   Of pure ablution round earth's human shores,
Or gazing on the new soft-fallen mask
   Of snow upon the mountains and the moors;
No—yet still steadfast, still unchangeable,
   Pillowed upon my fair love's ripening breast,
To feel for ever its soft fall and swell,
   Awake for ever in a sweet unrest,
Still, still to hear her tender-taken breath,
And so live ever—or else swoon to death.

JOHN KEATS

146   'Long time a child, and still a child,
                    when years'

❧❧❦·❧❧❦

LONG time a child, and still a child, when years
Had painted manhood on my cheek, was I;
For yet I lived like one not born to die;
A thriftless prodigal of smiles and tears,
No hope I needed, and I knew no fears.
But sleep, though sweet, is only sleep, and waking,
I waked to sleep no more, at once o'ertaking
The vanguard of my age, with all arrears
Of duty on my back. Nor child, nor man,
Nor youth, nor sage, I find my head is grey,
For I have lost the race I never ran,
A rathe December blights my lagging May;
And still I am a child, though I be old,
Time is my debtor for my years untold.

                              HARTLEY COLERIDGE

147 *Night*

THE crackling embers on the hearth are dead;
The indoor note of industry is still;
The latch is fast; upon the window sill
The small birds wait not for their daily bread;
The voiceless flowers—how quietly they shed
Their nightly odours;—and the household rill,
Murmurs continuous dulcet sounds that fill
The vacant expectation, and the dread
Of listening night. And haply now she sleeps;
For all the garrulous noises of the air
Are hushed in peace; the soft dew silent weeps,
Like hopeless lovers for a maid so fair—
Oh! that I were the happy dream that creeps
To her soft heart, to find my image there.

HARTLEY COLERIDGE

148   *Silence*

THERE is a silence where hath been no sound,
    There is a silence where no sound may be,
    In the cold grave—under the deep deep sea,
Or in wide desert where no life is found,
Which hath been mute, and still must sleep profound;
    No voice is hushed—no life treads silently,
    But clouds and cloudy shadows wander free,
That never spoke, over the idle ground:
But in green ruins, in the desolate walls
    Of antique palaces, where man hath been,
Though the dun fox, or wild hyena, calls,
    And owls, that flit continually between,
Shriek to the echo, and the low winds moan,
There the true silence is, self-conscious and alone.

                                    THOMAS HOOD

149   *To Vauxhall*

❧❧❧

'The English Garden.'—MASON

THE cold transparent ham is on my fork—
    It hardly rains—and hark the bell!—ding-dingle—
Away! Three thousand feet at gravel work
    Mocking a Vauxhall shower!—Married and single
Crush—rush;—soak'd silks with wet white satin mingle.
    Hengler! Madame! round whom all bright sparks lurk,
Calls audibly on Mr. and Mrs. Pringle
    To study the sublime, &c.—(vide Burke)
All noses are upturn'd—Whish—ish!—On high
    The rocket rushes—trails—just steals in sight—
Then droops and melts in bubbles of blue light—
    And darkness reigns—Then balls flare up and die—
Wheels whizz—smack crackers—serpents twist—and then
    Back to the cold transparent ham again!

THOMAS HOOD

150 *Literary Reminiscences*

> 'Dornton & Co. may challenge the world, the house of
> Hope perhaps excepted.'—*Road to Ruin*

TIME was, I sat upon a lofty stool
At lofty desk, and with a clerkly pen
Began each morning, at the stroke of ten,
To write in Bell & Co.'s commercial school;
In Warnford Court, a shady nook and cool,
The favourite retreat of merchant men;
Yet would my quill turn vagrant even then,
And take stray dips in the Castalian pool.
Now double entry—now a flowery trope—
Mingling poetic honey with trade wax—
Blogg, Brothers—Milton—Grote and Prescott—Pope—
Bristles—and Hogg—Glyn Mills and Halifax—
Rogers—and Towgood—Hemp—the Bard of Hope—
Barilla—Byron—Tallow—Burns—and Flax!

THOMAS HOOD

151   *False Friends-like*

WHEN I wer still a bwoy, an' mother's pride,
A bigger bwoy spoke up to me so kind-like,
'If you do like, I'll treat ye wi'a ride
In theäse wheel-barrow here.' Zoo I were blind-like
To what he had a-workèn in his mind-like,
An' mounted vor a passenger inside;
An' comèn to a puddle, perty wide,
He tipped me in, a-grinnèn back behind-like.
Zoo when a man do come to me so thick-like,
An' sheäke my hand, where woonce he passed me by,
An' tell me he would do me this or that,
I can't help thinkèn o' the big bwoy's trick-like.
An' then, vor all I can but wag my hat
An' thank en, I do veel a little shy.

WILLIAM BARNES

153

152 *To Tartar, a terrier beauty*

SNOWDROP of dogs, with ear of brownest dye,
Like the last orphan leaf of naked tree
Which shudders in bleak autumn; though by thee,
Of hearing careless and untutored eye,
Not understood articulate speech of men,
Nor marked the artificial mind of books,
—The mortal's voice eternized by the pen,—
Yet hast thou thought and language all unknown
To Babel's scholars; oft intensest looks,
Long scrutiny o'er some dark-veined stone
Dost thou bestow, learning dead mysteries
Of the world's birth-day, oft in eager tone
With quick-tailed fellows bandiest prompt replies,
Solicitudes canine, four-footed amities.

THOMAS LOVELL BEDDOES

153 *'If thou must love me, let it be for nought'*

IF thou must love me, let it be for nought
Except for love's sake only. Do not say
'I love her for her smile—her look—her way
Of speaking gently,—for a trick of thought
That falls in well with mine, and certes brought
A sense of pleasant ease on such a day'—
For these things in themselves, belovèd, may
Be changed, or change for thee,—and love, so wrought,
May be unwrought so. Neither love me for
Thine own dear pity's wiping my cheeks dry,—
A creature might forget to weep, who bore
Thy comfort long, and lose thy love thereby!
But love me for love's sake, that evermore
Thou may'st love on, through love's eternity.

ELIZABETH BARRETT BROWNING

154 *'I never gave a lock of hair away'*

I NEVER gave a lock of hair away
To a man, dearest, except this to thee,
Which now upon my fingers thoughtfully,
I ring out to the full brown length and say
'Take it.' My day of youth went yesterday;
My hair no longer bounds to my foot's glee,
Nor plant I it from rose or myrtle-tree,
As girls do, any more: it only may
Now shade on two pale cheeks the mark of tears,
Taught drooping from the head that hangs aside
Through sorrow's trick. I thought the funeral-shears
Would take this first, but love is justified, —
Take it thou, — finding pure, from all those years,
The kiss my mother left here when she died.

ELIZABETH BARRETT BROWNING

155 *'Say over again, and yet once over again'*

SAY over again, and yet once over again,
That thou dost love me. Though the word repeated
Should seem 'a cuckoo-song,' as thou dost treat it.
Remember, never to the hill or plain,
Valley and wood, without her cuckoo-strain
Comes the fresh Spring in all her green completed.
Belovèd, I, amid the darkness greeted
By a doubtful spirit-voice, in that doubt's pain
Cry, 'Speak once more—thou lovest!' Who can fear
Too many stars, though each in heaven shall roll,
Too many flowers, though each shall crown the year?
Say though dost love me, love me, love me—toll
The silver iterance!—only minding, dear,
To love me also in silence with thy soul.

ELIZABETH BARRETT BROWNING

156 *'How do I love thee? Let me count the ways'*

How do I love thee? Let me count the ways.
I love thee to the depth and breadth and height
My soul can reach, when feeling out of sight
For the ends of being and ideal grace.
I love thee to the level of everyday's
Most quiet need, by sun and candlelight.
I love thee freely, as men strive for right;
I love thee purely, as they turn from praise.
I love thee with the passion put to use
In my old griefs, and with my childhood's faith.
I love thee with a love I seemed to lose
With my lost saints, —I love thee with the breath,
Smiles, tears, of all my life! —and, if God choose,
I shall but love thee better after death.

ELIZABETH BARRETT BROWNING

157   *'Belovèd, thou hast brought me
              many flowers'*

❧❧❧

BELOVÈD, thou hast brought me many flowers
Plucked in the garden, all the summer through
And winter, and it seemed as if they grew
In this close room, nor missed the sun and showers.
So, in the like name of that love of ours,
Take back these thoughts which here unfolded too,
And which on warm and cold days I withdrew
From my heart's ground. Indeed, those beds and bowers
Be overgrown with bitter weeds and rue,
And wait thy weeding; yet here's eglantine,
Here's ivy!—take them, as I used to do
Thy flowers, and keep them where they shall not pine.
Instruct thine eyes to keep their colours true,
And tell thy soul, their roots are left in mine.

ELIZABETH BARRETT BROWNING

158 *The Galaxy*

TORRENT of light and river of the air,
  Along whose bed the glimmering stars are seen
  Like gold and silver sands in some ravine
  Where mountain streams have left their channels bare!
The Spaniard sees in thee the pathway, where
  His patron saint descended in the sheen
  Of his celestial armour, on serene
  And quiet nights, when all the heavens were fair.
Not this I see, nor yet the ancient fable
  Of Phaeton's wild course, that scorched the skies
  Where'er the hoofs of his hot coursers trod;
But the white drift of worlds o'er chasms of sable,
  The star-dust, that is whirled aloft and flies
  From the invisible chariot-wheels of God.

HENRY WADSWORTH LONGFELLOW

159   *The Broken Oar*

ONCE upon the Iceland's solitary strand
    A poet wandered with his book and pen,
    Seeking some final word, some sweet Amen,
    Wherewith to close the volume in his hand.
The billows rolled and plunged upon the sand,
    The circling sea-gulls swept beyond his ken,
    And from the parting cloud-rack now and then
    Flashed the red sunset over sea and land.
Then by the billows at his feet was tossed
    A broken oar; and carved thereon he read,
    'Oft was I weary, when I toiled at thee';
And like a man, who findeth what was lost,
    He wrote the words, then lifted up his head,
    And flung his useless pen into the sea.

HENRY WADSWORTH LONGFELLOW

160   *To a Cape Ann Schooner*

Luck to the craft that bears this name of mine,
Good fortune follow with her golden spoon
The glazèd hat and tarry pantaloon;
And wheresoe'er her keel shall cut the brine,
Cod, hake and haddock quarrel for her line.
Shipped with her crew, whatever wind may blow,
Or tides delay, my wish with her shall go,
Fishing by proxy. Would that it might show
At need her course, in lack of sun and star,
Where icebergs threaten, and the sharp reefs are;
Lift the blind fog on Anticosti's lee
And Avalon's rock; make populous the sea
Round Grand Manan with eager finny swarms,
Break the long calms, and charm away the storms.

JOHN GREENLEAF WHITTIER

161   *A Dream*

❧❧❧

I DREAM'D a morning dream—a torrent brought
From fruitless hills, was rushing deep and wide:
It ran in rapids, like impatient thought;
It wheel'd in eddies, like bewilder'd pride:
Bleak-faced Neology, in cap and gown,
Peer'd up the channel of the spreading tide,
As, with a starved expectancy, he cried,
'When will the Body of the Christ come down?'
He came—not It, but He! no rolling waif
Tost by the waves—no drown'd and helpless form—
But with unlapsing step, serene and safe,
As once He trod the waters in the storm;
The gownsman trembled as his God went by—
I look'd again, the torrent-bed was dry.

CHARLES TENNYSON TURNER

162   *East or West?*

I SAT within a window, looking west,
On a fair autumn eve; the forest leaves
Moved o'er a fiery sunset, vision blest
After that day of storm and rainy eaves.
While thus I gazed, I heard a sweet voice cry:—
'Come to the east, and see the rainbow die.
On the last shower anon the moon will rise,
And light the village when the rainbow dies.'
Betwixt the two I could not well decide;
For each was fair, and both would vanish soon.
But that sweet voice cried eastward still: I knew
No light would pierce the wood when day withdrew;
So I went east and to the rising moon
The village brightened when the rainbow died.

CHARLES TENNYSON TURNER

163   *Letty's Globe*

WHEN Letty had scarce passed her third glad year,
And her young, artless words began to flow,
One day we gave the child a coloured sphere
Of the wide earth, that she might mark and know,
By tint and outline, all its sea and land.
She patted all the world; old empires peeped
Between her baby fingers; her soft hand
Was welcome at all frontiers. How she leaped
And laughed, and prattled in her world-wide bliss;
But when we turned her sweet unlearned eye
On our own isle, she raised a joyous cry,
'Oh! yes, I see it, Letty's home is there!'
And, while she hid all England with a kiss,
Bright over Europe fell her golden hair.

                              CHARLES TENNYSON TURNER

164   *Great Britain through the Ice*
Or, Premature Patriotism

METHOUGHT I lived in the icy times forlorn;
And, with a fond forecasting love and pride,
I hung o'er frozen England:— 'When,' I cried,
'When will the island of our hopes be born?
When will our fields be seen, our church-bells heard?
And Avon, Doon, and Tweed break forth in song?
This blank unstoried ice be warmed and stirred,
And Thames, and Clyde, and Humber roll along
To a free sea-board? airs of paradise
Instal our summer and our flowery springs,
And lift the larks, and land the nightingales?
And this wild alien unfamiliar Wales
Melt home among her harps? and vernal skies
Thaw out old Dover for the houseless kings?'

CHARLES TENNYSON TURNER

165   *Julius Cæsar and the Honey-bee*

PORING on Cæsar's death with earnest eye,
I heard a fretful buzzing in the pane:
'Poor bee!' I cried, 'I'll help thee by-and-by;'
Then dropped mine eyes upon the page again.
Alas! I did not rise; I helped him not:
In the great voice of Roman history
I lost the pleading of the window-bee,
And all his woes and troubles were forgot.
In pity for the mighty chief, who bled
Beside his rival's statue, I delayed
To serve the little insect's present need;
And so he died for lack of human aid.
I could not change the Roman's destiny;
I might have set the honey-maker free.

CHARLES TENNYSON TURNER

166 *To Science*

SCIENCE! true daughter of Old Time thou art!
  Who alterest all things with thy peering eyes.
Why preyest thou thus upon the poet's heart,
  Vulture, whose wings are dull realities?
How should he love thee? or how deem thee wise,
  Who wouldst not leave him in his wandering
To seek for treasure in the jewelled skies,
  Albeit he soared with an undaunted wing?
Hast thou not dragged Diana from her car?
  And driven the hamadryad from the wood
To seek a shelter in some happier star?
  Hast thou not torn the naiad from her flood,
The elfin from the green grass, and from me
The summer dream beneath the tamarind tree?

EDGAR ALLAN POE

167 *Lines on Cambridge of 1830*

THEREFORE your Halls, your ancient Colleges,
Your portals statued with old kings and queens,
Your gardens, myriad-volumed libraries,
Wax-lighted chapels, and rich carven screens,
Your doctors, and your proctors, and your deans,
Shall not avail you, when the Day-beam sports
New-risen o'er awakened Albion. No!
Nor yet your solemn organ-pipes that blow
Melodious thunders through your vacant courts
At noon and eve, because your manner sorts
Not with this age wherefrom ye stand apart,
Because the lips of little children preach
Against you, you that do profess to teach
And teach us nothing, feeding not the heart.

ALFRED TENNYSON, LORD TENNYSON

168   *'If I were loved, as I desire to be'*

I F I were loved, as I desire to be,
What is there in the great sphere of the earth,
And range of evil between death and birth,
That I should fear,—if I were loved by thee?
All the inner, all the outer world of pain
Clear Love would pierce and cleave, if thou wert mine.
As I have heard that, somewhere in the main,
Fresh-water springs come up through bitter brine.
'Twere joy, not fear, claspt hand-in-hand with thee,
To wait for death—mute—careless of all ills,
Apart upon a mountain, though the surge
Of some new deluge from a thousand hills
Flung leagues of roaring foam into the gorge
Below us, as far on as eye could see.

ALFRED TENNYSON, LORD TENNYSON

169   *'How thought you that this thing could captivate?'*

❦❦❦

How thought you that this thing could captivate?
   What are those graces that could make her dear,
   Who is not worth the notice of a sneer
To rouse the vapid devil of her hate?
A speech conventional, so void of weight
   That after it has buzzed about one's ear,
   'Twere rich refreshment for a week to hear
The dentist babble or the barber prate;

A hand displayed with many a little art;
   An eye that glances on her neighbour's dress;
    A foot too often shown for my regard;
An angel's form—a waiting-woman's heart;
  A perfect-featured face, expressionless,
    Insipid, as the Queen upon a card.

ALFRED TENNYSON, LORD TENNYSON

170   *'Guess well, and that is well.*
Our age can find'

✻✾✻✾✻✾✻

GUESS well, and that is well. Our age can find
The shower that fell a million years ago,
An ever-vanished ocean's ebb and flow
Rock-written; but no man can send his mind
Into man's past so well, that he can form
A perfect likeness of long-vanished souls,
Whate'er new lights be let on ancient scrolls
And secular perforations of the worm.
Courage, old Clio! we have read the rocks,
You see the past dilated through the fog
Of ages. Do your best, for that remains.
More will you do. We are more than goat or ox,
More than the long-descended horse and dog,
Whose one dumb record is their limbs and brains.

ALFRED TENNYSON, LORD TENNYSON

171   *Continuity of Life*

Nay, let me own it is but vain regret,
    Not wise, to disavow life's unity,
    To cry out, Oh, it was a child, not I,
It was a boy, it was a lover's fret
Caught in the magic of a golden net,
    It was a run-away tracked by a hound
    He needs must slay, must tread into the ground,—
Groping about to find some oubliette.

It was the very self, the self indeed,
    Said the true word or thought the treacherous thought;
The very self fate-driven, did the deed
    That won the prize, or black-crowned doomster brought:
And thus it is we look beyond the shore
That girds our isle, while Hope flies on before.

                            WILLIAM BELL SCOTT

172   *The Names*

(*To Shakespeare*)

SHAKESPEARE! —to such name's sounding what succeeds
    Fitly as silence? Falter forth the spell,—
    Act follows word, the speaker knows full well,
Nor tampers with its magic more than needs.
Two names there are: That which the Hebrew reads
    With his soul only: if from lips it fell,
    Echo, back thundered by earth, heaven and hell,
Would own 'Thou did'st create us!' Nought impedes
We voice the other name, man's most of might,
    Awesomely, lovingly: let awe and love
Mutely await their working, leave to sight
    All of the issue as— below—above—
Shakespeare's creation rises: one remove,
Though dread—this finite from that infinite.

ROBERT BROWNING

173 *Now*

Out of your whole life give but a moment!
All of your life that has gone before,
All to come after it,—so you ignore
So you make perfect the present,—condense,
In a rapture of rage, for perfection's endowment,
Thought and feeling and soul and sense—
Merged in a moment which gives me at last
You around me for once, you beneath me, above me—
Me—sure that despite of time future, time past,—
This tick of our life-time's one moment you love me!
How long such suspension may linger? Ah, sweet—
The moment eternal—just that and no more—
When ecstasy's utmost we clutch at the core
While cheeks burn, arms open, eyes shut and lips meet!

ROBERT BROWNING

174 *To Britain*

By the D—— of W——

❧❧❧

HALT! Shoulder arms! Recover! As you were!
    Right wheel! Eyes left! Attention! Stand at ease!
O Britain! O my country! Words like these
    Have made thy name a terror and a fear
To all the nations. Witness Ebro's banks,
    Assaye, Toulouse, Nivelle, and Waterloo,
    Where the grim despot muttered—*Sauve qui peut!*
And Ney fled darkling.—Silence in the ranks!
Inspired by these, amidst the iron crash
    Of armies, in the centre of his troop
The soldier stands—unmovable, not rash—
    Until the forces of the foeman droop;
Then knocks the Frenchmen to eternal smash,
    Pounding them into mummy. Shoulder, hoop!

WILLIAM EDMONDSTONE AYTOUN

175 ## 'Though to the vilest things
beneath the moon'

THOUGH to the vilest things beneath the moon
For poor ease' sake I give away my heart,
And for the moment's sympathy let part
My sight and sense of truth, Thy precious boon,
My painful earnings, lost, all lost, as soon,
Almost, as gained: and though aside I start,
Belie Thee daily, hourly, — still Thou art,
Art surely as in heaven the sun at noon;
How much so e'er I sin, whate'er I do
Of evil, still the sky above is blue,
The stars look down in beauty as before:
It is enough to walk as best we may,
To walk, and sighing, dream of that blest day
When ill we cannot quell shall be no more.

ARTHUR HUGH CLOUGH

176 *'An upper chamber in a darkened house'*

An upper chamber in a darkened house,
Where, ere his footsteps reached ripe manhood's brink,
Terror and anguish were his lot to drink;
I cannot rid the thought nor hold it close
But dimly dream upon that man alone:
Now though the autumn clouds most softly pass,
The cricket chides beneath the doorstep stone
And greener than the season grows the grass.
Nor can I drop my lids nor shade my brows,
But there he stands beside the lifted sash;
And with a swooning of the heart, I think
Where the black shingles slope to meet the boughs
And, shattered on the roof like smallest snows,
The tiny petals of the mountain ash.

FREDERICK GODDARD TUCKERMAN

177   *'Tall stately plants with spikes and forks of gold'*

TALL stately plants with spikes and forks of gold
Crowd every slope: my heart repeats its cry,
A cry for strength, for strength and victory:
The will to strive, the courage overbold
That would have moved me once to turn indeed
And level with the dust each lordly weed.
But now I weep upon my wayside walks
And sigh for those fair days, when glorying
I stood a boy amid the mullein-stalks
And wished myself like him the Lion King:
There, where his shield shed arrows and his helm
Rang like a bell beaten with axe and brand,
He pushed the battle backward, realm on realm
Fallen in the swordswing of his stormy hand.

FREDERICK GODDARD TUCKERMAN

178 *Shakespeare*

OTHERS abide our question. Thou art free.
We ask and ask—Thou smilest and art still,
Out-topping knowledge. For the loftiest hill,
Who to the stars uncrowns his majesty,

Planting his steadfast footsteps in the sea,
Making the heaven of heavens his dwelling-place,
Spares but the cloudy border of his base
To the foiled searching of mortality;

And thou, who didst the stars and sunbeams know,
Self-schooled, self-scanned, self-honoured, self-secure,
Didst tread on earth unguessed at.—Better so!

All pains the immortal spirit must endure,
All weakness which impairs, all griefs which bow,
Find their sole speech in that victorious brow.

MATTHEW ARNOLD

179   *Written in Butler's Sermons*

AFFECTIONS, Instincts, Principles, and Powers,
Impulse and Reason, Freedom and Control—
So men, unravelling God's harmonious whole,
Rend in a thousand shreds this life of ours.

Vain labour! Deep and broad, where none may see,
Spring the foundations of that shadowy throne
Where man's one nature, queen-like, sits alone,
Centred in a majestic unity;

And rays her powers, like sister-islands seen
Linking their coral arms under the sea,
Or clustered peaks with plunging gulfs between

Spanned by aërial arches all of gold,
Where'er the chariot wheels of life are rolled
In cloudy circles to eternity.

MATTHEW ARNOLD

180 *To the Hungarian Nation*

NOT in sunk Spain's prolonged death agony;
Not in rich England, bent but to make pour
The flood of the world's commerce on her shore;
Not in that madhouse, France, from whence the cry
Afflicts grave Heaven with its long senseless roar;
Not in American vulgarity,
Nor wordy German imbecility—
Lies any hope of heroism more.
Hungarians! Save the world! Renew the stories
Of men who against hope repelled the chain,
And make the world's dead spirit leap again!
On land renew that Greek exploit, whose glories
Hallow the Salaminian promontories,
And the Armada flung to the fierce main.

MATTHEW ARNOLD

181 *Preparation*

Too weak am I to pray, as some have prayed,
That love might hurry straightway out of mind,
And leave an ever-vacant waste behind.
I thank thee rather, that through every grade
Of less and less affection we decline,
As month by month thy strong importunate fate
Thrusts back my claims, and draws thee toward the great,
And shares amongst a hundred what was mine.
Proud heroes ask to perish in high noon:
I'd have refractions of the fallen day,
And heavings when the gale hath flown away,
And this slow disenchantment: since too soon,
Too surely, comes the death of my poor heart,
Be it inured to pain, in mercy, ere we part.

WILLIAM CORY

182 ## *In a Spring Grove*

HERE the white-rayed anemone is born,
Wood-sorrel, and the varnished buttercup;
And primrose in its purfled green swathed up,
Pallid and sweet round every budding thorn,
Gray ash, and beech with rusty leaves outworn.
  Here, too, the darting linnet hath her nest
In the blue-lustered holly, never shorn,
    Whose partner cheers her little brooding breast,
Piping from some near bough. O simple song!
O cistern deep of that harmonious rillet,
And these fair juicy stems that climb and throng
    The vernal world, and unexhausted seas
Of flowing life, and soul that asks to fill it,
    Each and all these,—and more, and more than these!

WILLIAM ALLINGHAM

183 *In Snow*

O ENGLISH mother, in the ruddy glow
Hugging your baby closer when outside
You see the silent, soft, and cruel snow
Falling again, and think what ills betide
Unsheltered creatures,—your sad thoughts may go
Where War and Winter now, two spectre-wolves,
Hunt in the freezing vapour that involves
Those Asian peaks of ice and gulfs below.
Does this young soldier heed the snow that fills
His mouth and open eyes? or mind, in truth,
To-night, *his* mother's parting syllables?
Ha! is't a red coat?—Merely blood. Keep ruth
For others; this is but an Afghan youth
Shot by the stranger on his native hills.

WILLIAM ALLINGHAM

184   *Liberty to M. le Diplomate*

THOU fool who treatest with the sword, and not
With the strong arm that wields it! Thou insane
Who seest the dew-drops on the lion's mane,
But dost forget the lion! Oh thou sot,
Hugging thy drunken dream! Thou idiot
Who makest a covenant against the rain
With autumn leaves! Thou atheist who dost chain
This miserable body that can rot,
And thinkest it Me! Fool! for the swordless arm
Shall strike thee dead. Madman, the lion wakes,
And with one shake is dry. Sot, the day breaks
Shall sober even thee. Idiot, one storm
And thou art bare. Atheist, the corse is thine,
But lo, the unfettered soul immortal and divine!

                                        SIDNEY DOBELL

185 *Lucifer in Starlight*

ᏅᏅᏅ

On a starred night Prince Lucifer uprose.
Tired of his dark dominion swung the fiend
Above the rolling ball in cloud part screened,
Where sinners hugged their spectre of repose.
Poor prey to his hot fit of pride were those.
And now upon his western wing he leaned,
Now his huge bulk o'er Afric's sands careened,
Now the black planet shadowed Arctic snows.
Soaring through wider zones that pricked his scars
With memory of the old revolt from Awe,
He reached a middle height, and at the stars,
Which are the brain of heaven, he looked, and sank.
Around the ancient track marched rank on rank,
The army of unalterable law.

GEORGE MEREDITH

186–7 *Camelus Saltat*

WHAT say you, critic, now you have become
An author and maternal?—in this trap
(To quote you) of poor hollow folk who rap
On instruments as like as drum to drum.
You snarled tut-tut for welcome to tum-tum,
So like the nose fly-teased in its noon's nap.
You scratched an insect-slaughtering thunder-clap
With that between the fingers and the thumb.
It seemeth mad to quit the Olympian couch,
Which bade our public gobble or reject.
O spectacle of Peter, shrewdly pecked,
Piper, by his own pepper from his pouch!
What of the sneer, the jeer, the voice austere,
You dealt?—the voice austere, the jeer, the sneer.

Camelus Saltat (continued)

ORACLE of the market! thence you drew
The taste which stamped you guide of the inept.—
A North-sea pilot, Hildebrand yclept,
A sturdy and a briny, once men knew.
He loved small beer, and for that copious brew,
To roll ingurgitation till he slept,
Rations exchanged with flavour for the adept:
And merrily plied him captain, mate and crew.
At last this dancer to the Polar star
Sank, washed out within, and overboard was pitched,
To drink the sea and pilot him to land.
O captain-critic! printed, neatly stitched,
Know, while the pillory-eggs fly fast, they are
Not eggs, but the drowned soul of Hildebrand.

GEORGE MEREDITH

188–91   *Willowwood*

❧❧ i ❧❧

I SAT with Love upon a woodside well,
   Leaning across the water, I and he;
   Nor ever did he speak nor looked at me,
But touched his lute wherein was audible
The certain secret thing he had to tell:
   Only our mirrored eyes met silently
   In the low wave; and that sound came to be
The passionate voice I knew; and my tears fell.

And at their fall, his eyes beneath grew hers;
And with his foot and with his wing-feathers
   He swept the spring that watered my heart's drouth.
Then the dark ripples spread to waving hair,
And as I stooped, her own lips rising there
   Bubbled with brimming kisses at my mouth.

❦❧ ii ❦❧

AND now Love sang: but his was such a song,
 So meshed with half-remembrance hard to free,
 As souls disused in death's sterility
May sing when the new birthday tarries long.
And I was made aware of a dumb throng
 That stood aloof, one form by every tree,
 All mournful forms, for each was I or she,
The shades of those our days that had no tongue.

They looked on us, and knew us and were known;
 While fast together, alive from the abyss,
 Clung the soul-wrung implacable close kiss;
And pity of self through all made broken moan
Which said, 'For once, for once, for once alone!'
 And still Love sang, and what he sang was this:—

꧁ iii ꧂

'O YE, all ye that walk in Willowwood,
    That walk with hollow faces burning white;
What fathom-depth of soul-struck widowhood,
    What long, what longer hours, one lifelong night,
Ere ye again, who so in vain have wooed
    Your last hope lost, who so in vain invite
Your lips to that their unforgotten food,
    Ere ye, ere ye again shall see the light!

Alas! the bitter banks in Willowwood,
    With tear-spurge wan, with blood-wort burning red:
Alas! if ever such a pillow could
    Steep deep the soul in sleep till she were dead,—
Better all life forget her than this thing,
That Willowwood should hold her wandering!'

❧❧❧ iv ❧❧❧

So sang he: and as meeting rose and rose
   Together cling through the wind's wellaway,
   Nor change at once, yet near the end of day
The leaves drop loosened where the heart-stain glows,—
So when the song died did the kiss unclose;
   And her face fell back drowned, and was as grey
   As its grey eyes; and if it ever may
Meet mine again I know not if Love knows.

Only I know that I leaned low and drank
A long draught from the water where she sank,
   Her breath and all her tears and all her soul:
And as I leaned, I know I felt Love's face
Pressed on my neck with moan of pity and grace,
   Till both our heads were in his aureole.

DANTE GABRIEL ROSSETTI

192 *He and I*

WHENCE came his feet into my field, and why?
   How is it that he sees it all so drear?
   How do I see his seeing, and how hear
The name his bitter silence knows it by?
This was the little fold of separate sky
   Whose pasturing clouds in the soul's atmosphere
   Drew living light from one continual year:
How should he find it lifeless? He, or I?

Lo! this new Self now wanders round my field,
   With plaints for every flower, and for each tree
   A moan, the sighing wind's auxiliary:
And o'er sweet waters of my life, that yield
Unto his lips no draught but tears unsealed,
   Even in my place he weeps. Even I, not he.

DANTE GABRIEL ROSSETTI

193–206   *Monna Innominata*

A Sonnet of Sonnets

Beatrice, immortalized by 'altissimo poeta ... cotanto amante';
Laura, celebrated by a great though an inferior bard,— have alike
paid the exceptional penalty of exceptional honour, and have
come down to us resplendent with charms, but (at least, to my
apprehension) scant of attractiveness.

These heroines of world-wide fame were preceded by a bevy of
unnamed ladies 'donne innominate' sung by a school of less
conspicuous poets; and in that land and that period which
gave simultaneous birth to Catholics, to Albigenses, and to
Troubadours, one can imagine many a lady as sharing her lover's
poetic aptitude, while the barrier between them might be one
held sacred by both, yet not such as to render mutual love incom-
patible with mutual honour.

Had such a lady spoken for herself, the portrait left us might
have appeared more tender, if less dignified, than any drawn even
by a devoted friend. Or had the Great Poetess of our own day and
nation only been unhappy instead of happy, her circumstances
would have invited her to bequeath to us, in lieu of the
'Portuguese Sonnets,' an inimitable 'donna innominata' drawn
not from fancy but from feeling, and worthy to occupy a niche
beside Beatrice and Laura.

❦ i ❦

'Lo dì che han detto a' dolci amici addio.'—DANTE
'Amor, con quanto sforzo oggi mi vinci!'—PETRARCA

COME back to me, who wait and watch for you:—
   Or come not yet, for it is over then,
   And long it is before you come again,
So far between my pleasures are and few.
While, when you come not, what I do I do
   Thinking 'Now when he comes,' my sweetest 'when:'
   For one man is my world of all the men
This wide world holds; O love, my world is you.
Howbeit, to meet you grows almost a pang
   Because the pang of parting comes so soon;
   My hope hangs waning, waxing, like a moon
      Between the heavenly days on which we meet:
Ah me, but where are now the songs I sang
   When life was sweet because you called them sweet?

❦ ii ❦

'Era già l'ora che volge il desio.'—DANTE
'Ricorro al tempo ch'io vi vidi prima.'—PETRARCA

I WISH I could remember, that first day,
　　First hour, first moment of your meeting me,
　　If bright or dim the season, it might be
Summer or Winter for aught that I can say;
So unrecorded did it slip away,
　　So blind was I to see and to foresee,
　　So dull to mark the budding of my tree
That would not blossom yet for many a May.
If only I could recollect it, such
　　A day of days! I let it come and go
　　As traceless as a thaw of bygone snow;
It seemed to mean so little, meant so much;
If only now I could recall that touch,
　　First touch of hand in hand—Did one but know!

❀❀❀ iii ❀❀❀

'O ombre vane, fuor che ne l'aspetto!'—DANTE
'Immaginata guida la conduce.'—PETRARCA

I DREAM of you to wake: would that I might
   Dream of you and not wake but slumber on;
   Nor find with dreams the dear companion gone,
As Summer ended Summer birds take flight.
In happy dreams I hold you full in sight,
   I blush again who waking look so wan;
   Brighter than sunniest day that ever shone,
In happy dreams your smile makes day of night.
Thus only in a dream we are at one,
   Thus only in a dream we give and take
     The faith that maketh rich who take or give;
If thus to sleep is sweeter than to wake,
     To die were surely sweeter than to live,
Though there be nothing new beneath the sun.

❧ iv ❧

'Poca favilla gran fiamma seconda.'—DANTE
'Ogni altra cosa, ogni pensier va fore,
E sol ivi con voi rimansi amore.'—PETRARCA

I LOVED you first: but afterwards your love
   Outsoaring mine, sang such a loftier song
As drowned the friendly cooings of my dove.
   Which owes the other most? my love was long,
   And yours one moment seemed to wax more strong;
I loved and guessed at you, you construed me
And loved me for what might or might not be—
   Nay, weights and measures do us both a wrong.
For verily love knows not 'mine' or 'thine;'
   With separate 'I' and 'thou' free love has done,
    For one is both and both are one in love:
Rich love knows nought of 'thine that is not mine;'
    Both have the strength and both the length thereof,
   Both of us, of the love which makes us one.

'Amor che a nulla amato amar perdona.'—DANTE
'Amor m'addusse in sì gioiosa spene.'—PETRARCA

O MY heart's heart, and you who are to me
   More than myself myself, God be with you,
   Keep you in strong obedience leal and true
To Him whose noble service setteth free,
Give you all good we see or can foresee,
   Make your joys many and your sorrows few,
   Bless you in what you bear and what you do,
Yea, perfect you as He would have you be.
So much for you; but what for me, dear friend?
   To love you without stint and all I can
Today, tomorrow, world without an end;
      To love you much and yet to love you more,
   As Jordan at his flood sweeps either shore;
Since woman is the helpmeet made for man.

❧❧❧ vi ❧❧❧

'Or puoi la quantitate
Comprender de l'amor che a te mi scalda.'—DANTE
'Non vo'che da tal nodo amor mi scioglia.'—PETRARCA

TRUST me, I have not earned your dear rebuke,
   I love, as you would have me, God the most;
   Would lose not Him, but you, must one be lost,
Nor with Lot's wife cast back a faithless look
Unready to forego what I forsook;
   This say I, having counted up the cost,
   This, though I be the feeblest of God's host,
The sorriest sheep Christ shepherds with His crook.
Yet while I love my God the most, I deem
   That I can never love you overmuch;
      I love Him more, so let me love you too;
   Yea, as I apprehend it, love is such
I cannot love you if I love not Him,
      I cannot love Him if I love not you.

❦❦❦ vii ❦❦❦

'Qui primavera sempre ed ogni frutto.'—DANTE
'Ragionando con meco ed io con lui.'—PETRARCA

'LOVE me, for I love you'—and answer me,
　　'Love me, for I love you'—so shall we stand
　　As happy equals in the flowering land
Of love, that knows not a dividing sea.
Love builds the house on rock and not on sand,
　　Love laughs what while the winds rave desperately;
And who hath found love's citadel unmanned?
　　And who hath held in bonds love's liberty?
My heart's a coward though my words are brave—
　　We meet so seldom, yet we surely part
　　So often; there's a problem for your art!
　　　Still I find comfort in his Book, who saith,
Though jealousy be cruel as the grave,
　　And death be strong, yet love is strong as death.

❦❦❦ viii ❦❦❦

'Come dicesse a Dio: D'altro non calme.'—DANTE
'Spero trovar pietà non che perdono.'—PETRARCA

'I, IF I perish, perish'—Esther spake:
　　And bride of life or death she made her fair
　　In all the lustre of her perfumed hair
And smiles that kindle longing but to slake.
She put on pomp of loveliness, to take
　　Her husband through his eyes at unaware;
　　She spread abroad her beauty for a snare,
Harmless as doves and subtle as a snake.
She trapped him with one mesh of silken hair,
　　She vanquished him by wisdom of her wit,
　　　　And built her people's house that it should stand:—
　　　　If I might take my life so in my hand,
And for my love to Love put up my prayer,
　　And for love's sake by Love be granted it!

❧ ix ❧

'O dignitosa coscienza e netta!'—DANTE
'Spirto più acceso di virtuti ardenti.'—PETRARCA

THINKING of you, and all that was, and all
   That might have been and now can never be,
   I feel your honoured excellence, and see
Myself unworthy of the happier call:
For woe is me who walk so apt to fall,
   So apt to shrink afraid, so apt to flee,
   Apt to lie down and die (ah, woe is me!)
Faithless and hopeless turning to the wall.
And yet not hopeless quite nor faithless quite,
Because not loveless; love may toil all night,
   But take at morning; wrestle till the break
      Of day, but then wield power with God and man:—
      So take I heart of grace as best I can,
   Ready to spend and be spent for your sake.

❧❧❧ X ❧❧❧

'Con miglior corso e con migliore stella.' —DANTE
'La vita fugge e non s'arresta un' ora.' —PETRARCA

TIME flies, hope flags, life plies a wearied wing;
   Death following hard on life gains ground apace;
   Faith runs with each and rears an eager face,
Outruns the rest, makes light of everything,
Spurns earth, and still finds breath to pray and sing;
   While love ahead of all uplifts his praise,
   Still asks for grace and still gives thanks for grace,
Content with all day brings and night will bring.
Life wanes; and when love folds his wings above
   Tired hope, and less we feel his conscious pulse,
     Let us fall asleep, dear friend, in peace:
     A little while, and age and sorrow cease;
   A little while, and life reborn annuls
Loss and decay and death, and all is love.

❧❧❧ xi ❧❧❧

'Vien dietro a me e lascia dir le genti.'—DANTE
'Contando i casi della vita nostra.'—PETRARCA

MANY in aftertimes will say of you
   'He loved her'—while of me what will they say?
   Not that I loved you more than just in play,
For fashion's sake as idle women do.
Even let them prate; who know not what we knew
   Of love and parting in exceeding pain,
   Of parting hopeless here to meet again,
Hopeless on earth, and heaven is out of view.
But by my heart of love laid bare to you,
   My love that you can make not void nor vain,
Love that foregoes you but to claim anew
     Beyond this passage of the gate of death,
   I charge you at the Judgment make it plain
     My love of you was life and not a breath.

❧❧❧ xii ❧❧❧

'Amor, che ne la mente mi ragiona.'—DANTE
'Amor vien nel bel viso di costei.'—PETRARCA

IF there be any one can take my place
   And make you happy whom I grieve to grieve,
   Think not that I can grudge it, but believe
I do commend you to that nobler grace,
That readier wit than mine, that sweeter face;
   Yea, since your riches make me rich, conceive
   I too am crowned, while bridal crowns I weave,
And thread the bridal dance with jocund pace.
For if I did not love you, it might be
   That I should grudge you some one dear delight;
    But since the heart is yours that was mine own,
   Your pleasure is my pleasure, right my right,
Your honourable freedom makes me free,
    And you companioned I am not alone.

◆◆◆ xiii ◆◆◆

'E drizzeremo glí occhi al Primo Amore.'—DANTE
'Ma trovo peso non da le mie braccia.'—PETRARCA

IF I could trust mine own self with your fate,
　　Shall I not rather trust it in God's hand?
　　Without Whose Will one lily doth not stand,
Nor sparrow fall at his appointed date;
　　Who numbereth the innumerable sand,
Who weighs the wind and water with a weight,
To Whom the world is neither small nor great,
　　Whose knowledge foreknew every plan we planned.
Searching my heart for all that touches you,
　　I find there only love and love's goodwill
Helpless to help and impotent to do,
　　　　Of understanding dull, of sight most dim;
　　　　And therefore I commend you back to Him
　　Whose love your love's capacity can fill.

❧❧❧ xiv ❧❧❧

'E la Sua Volontade è nostra pace.'—DANTE
'Sol con questi pensier, con altre chiome.'—PETRARCA

YOUTH gone, and beauty gone if ever there
   Dwelt beauty in so poor a face as this;
   Youth gone and beauty, what remains of bliss?
I will not bind fresh roses in my hair,
To shame a cheek at best but little fair,—
   Leave youth his roses, who can bear a thorn,—
I will not seek for blossoms anywhere,
   Except such common flowers as blow with corn.
Youth gone and beauty gone, what doth remain?
   The longing of a heart pent up forlorn,
     A silent heart whose silence loves and longs;
     The silence of a heart which sang its songs
   While youth and beauty made a summer morn,
Silence of love that cannot sing again.

CHRISTINA ROSSETTI

207–9   *'She was too kind, wooed too*
persistently'

❧❧❧ i ❧❧❧

SHE was too kind, wooed too persistently,
Wrote moving letters to me day by day;
The more she wrote, the more unmoved was I,
The more she gave, the less could I repay.
Therefore I grieve, not that I was not loved,
But that, being loved, I could not love again.
I liked, but like and love are far removed;
Hard though I tried to love I tried in vain.
For she was plain and lame and fat and short,
Forty and over-kind. Hence it befell
That though I loved her in a certain sort,
Yet did I love too wisely but not well.
    Ah! had she been more beauteous or less kind
    She might have found me of another mind.

ii

AND now, though twenty years are come and gone,
That little lame lady's face is with me still;
Never a day but what, on every one,
She dwells with me, as dwell she ever will.
She said she wished I knew not wrong from right;
It was not that; I knew, and would have chosen
Wrong if I could, but, in my own despite,
Power to choose wrong in my chilled veins was frozen.
'Tis said that if a woman woo, no man
Should leave her till she have prevailed; and, true,
A man will yield for pity, if he can,
But if the flesh rebels what can he do?
    I could not. Hence I grieve my whole life long
    The wrong I did, in that I did no wrong.

⟐ iii ⟐

Had I been some young sailor, continent
Perforce three weeks and then well plied with wine,
I might in time have tried to yield consent
And almost (though I doubt it) made her mine.
Or had it been but once and never again,
Come what come might, she should have had her way;
But yielding once were yielding twice, and then
I had been hers for ever and a day.
Or had she only been content to crave
A marriage of true minds, her wish was granted;
My mind was hers, I was her willing slave
In all things else except the one she wanted:
    And here, alas! at any rate to me
    She was an all too, too impossible she.

SAMUEL BUTLER

210   *'Record is nothing, and the hero great'*

RECORD is nothing, and the hero great
Without it; the vitality of fame
Is more than monument or fading state
That leaves us but the echo of a name.

Rumour, imperial mistress of the time,
Is slandered where she feigns no specious lies,
Caters no reticence of cringing rhyme,
To blow her dust-cloud full on unborn eyes—

The glory of the shows of gilded shields,
Wild music, fluttering blazons,—and 'tis all.
Lonely the dead men stare on battlefields,—
Can glory reach them now though clarions call?

Some shadow of their onset's broken gleam
May yet outlast the pageant and the dream.

JOHN LEICESTER WARREN,
BARON DE TABLEY

211 *Love and Sleep*

LYING asleep between the strokes of night
  I saw my love lean over my sad bed,
  Pale as the duskiest lily's leaf or head,
Smooth-skinned and dark, with bare throat made to bite,
Too wan for blushing and too warm for white,
  But perfect-coloured without white or red.
  And her lips opened amorously, and said—
I wist not what, saving one word—Delight.
And all her face was honey to my mouth,
  And all her body pasture to mine eyes;
    The long lithe arms and hotter hands than fire,
The quivering flanks, hair smelling of the south,
  The bright light feet, the splendid supple thighs
    And glittering eyelids of my soul's desire.

ALGERNON CHARLES SWINBURNE

212   *On the Russian persecution of the Jews*

O son of man, by lying tongues adored,
    By slaughterous hands of slaves with feet red-shod
    In carnage deep as ever Christian trod
Profaned with prayer and sacrifice abhorred
And incense from the trembling tyrant's horde,
    Brute worshippers or wielders of the rod,
    Most murderous even of all that call thee God,
Most treacherous even that ever called thee Lord;
Face loved of little children long ago,
    Head hated of the priests and rulers then,
        If thou see this, or hear these hounds of thine
        Run ravening as the Gadarean swine,
Say, was not this thy Passion, to foreknow
    In death's worst hour the works of Christian men?

January 23, 1882

ALGERNON CHARLES SWINBURNE

215

213 *For a Picture*

T H AT nose is out of drawing. With a gasp,
    She pants upon the passionate lips that ache
    With the red drain of her own mouth, and make
A monochord of colour. Like an asp,
One lithe lock wriggles in his rutilant grasp.
    Her bosom is an oven of myrrh, to bake
    Love's white warm shewbread to a browner cake.
The lock his fingers clench has burst its hasp.
The legs are absolutely abominable.
    Ah! what keen overgust of wild-eyed woes
    Flags in that bosom, flushes in that nose?
Nay! Death sets riddles for desire to spell,
    Responsive. What red hem earth's passion sews,
But may be ravenously unripped in hell?

ALGERNON CHARLES SWINBURNE

214   *Mother and Daughter*

SHE will not have it that my day wanes low,
    Poor of the fire its drooping sun denies,
    That on my brow the thin lines write good-byes
Which soon may be read plain for all to know,
Telling that I have done with youth's brave show;
    Alas! and done with youth in heart and eyes,
    With wonder and with far expectancies,
Save but to say 'I knew such long ago.'

She will not have it. Loverlike to me,
    She with her happy gaze finds all that's best,
She sees this fair and that unfretted still,
    And her own sunshine over all the rest:
So she half keeps me as she'd have me be,
And I forget to age, through her sweet will.

AUGUSTA WEBSTER

215 *'Farewell, then. It is finished. I forego'*

FAREWELL, then. It is finished. I forego
With this all right in you, even that of tears.
If I have spoken hardly, it will show
How much I loved you. With you disappears
A glory, a romance of many years.
What you may be henceforth I will not know.
The phantom of your presence on my fears
Is impotent at length for weal or woe.
Your past, your present, all alike must fade
In a new land of dreams where love is not.
Then kiss me and farewell. The choice is made
And we shall live to see the past forgot,
If not forgiven. See, I came to curse,
Yet stay to bless. I know not which is worse.

WILFRID SCAWEN BLUNT

216   *Hap*

❧❧❧❧

I f but some vengeful god would call to me
From up the sky, and laugh: 'Thou suffering thing,
Know that thy sorrow is my ecstasy,
That thy love's loss is my hate's profiting!'

Then would I bear it, clench myself, and die,
Steeled by the sense of ire unmerited;
Half-eased in that a Powerfuller than I
Had willed and meted me the tears I shed.

But not so. How arrives it joy lies slain,
And why unblooms the best hope ever sown?
—Crass Casualty obstructs the sun and rain,
And dicing Time for gladness casts a moan. . . .
These purblind Doomsters had as readily strown
Blisses about my pilgrimage as pain.

THOMAS HARDY

217 *The Sleep-worker*

WHEN wilt thou wake, O Mother, wake and see—
As one who, held in trance, has laboured long
By vacant rote and prepossession strong—
The coils that thou hast wrought unwittingly;

Wherein have place, unrealized by thee,
Fair growths, foul cankers, right enmeshed with wrong.
Strange orchestras of victim-shriek and song,
And curious blends of ache and ecstasy?—

Should that morn come, and show thy opened eyes
All that Life's palpitating tissues feel,
How wilt thou bear thyself in thy surprise?—

Wilt thou destroy, in one wild shock of shame,
Thy whole high heaving firmamental frame,
Or patiently adjust, amend, and heal?

THOMAS HARDY

218   *The Minute before Meeting*

THE grey gaunt days dividing us in twain
Seemed hopeless hills my strength must faint to climb,
But they are gone; and now I would detain
The few clock-beats that part us; rein back Time,

And live in close expectance never closed
In change for far expectance closed at last,
So harshly has expectance been imposed
On my long need while these slow blank months passed.

And knowing that what is now about to be
Will all *have been* in oh, so short a space!
I read beyond it my despondency
When more dividing months shall take its place,
Thereby denying to this hour of grace
A full-up measure of felicity.

THOMAS HARDY

219 ## *A Church Romance*

(*Mellstock: circa 1835*)

SHE turned in the high pew, until her sight
Swept the west gallery, and caught its row
Of music-men with viol, book, and bow
Against the sinking sad tower-window light.

She turned again; and in her pride's despite
One strenuous viol's inspirer seemed to throw
A message from his string to her below,
Which said: 'I claim thee as my own forthright!'

Thus their hearts' bond began, in due time signed.
And long years thence, when Age had scared Romance,
At some old attitude of his or glance
That gallery-scene would break upon her mind,
With him as minstrel, ardent, young, and trim,
Bowing 'New Sabbath' or 'Mount Ephraim.'

THOMAS HARDY

220   *The Wanderers*

GOD's blessing on poor ship-folk! Peace and prayer
    Fall on their eyelids till they close in sleep!
God send them gentle winds and summer air,
    For the great sea is treacherous and deep.
    Light me up lamps on every ocean-steep,—
Beacon the shallows with a loving care.
    Ay me! the wind cries and the wild waves leap,
And on they drive—God knows—*they* know not—where.
    Come poets! come, O prophets! yea, disown
The phantasies and phantoms ye pursue!
    Lights! lights! with fatal snares the sea is sown.
Guide the poor ship-folk lone beneath the blue.
    Nay, do not light for Lazarus alone,
But light for Dives and the Devil too.

ROBERT BUCHANAN

221　　　　　　　　*The Singer*

'THAT was the thrush's last good-night,' I thought,
And heard the soft descent of summer rain
In the drooped garden leaves; but hush! again
The perfect iterance,—freer than unsought
Odours of violets dim in woodland ways,
Deeper than coilèd waters laid a-dream
Below mossed ledges of a shadowy stream,
And faultless as blown roses in June days.
Full-throated singer! art thou thus anew
Voiceful to hear how round thyself alone
The enrichèd silence drops for thy delight
More soft than snow, more sweet than honey-dew?
Now cease: the last faint western streak is gone,
Stir not the blissful quiet of the night.

EDWARD DOWDEN

222 *To Francis Jammes*

❦❦❦

'TIS April again in my garden, again the grey stone-wall
   Is prankt with yellow alyssum and lilac aubrey-cresses;
   Half-hidden the mavis caroleth in the tassely birchen tresses
And awhile on the sunny air a cuckoo tuneth his call:
Now cometh to mind a singer whom country joys enthral,
   Francis Jammes, so grippeth him Nature in her caresses
   She hath steeped his throat in the honeyed air of her
      wildernesses
With beauty that countervails the Lutetian therewithal.

You are here in spirit, dear poet, and bring a motley group,
   Your friends, afore you sat stitching your heavenly
      trousseau—
   The courteous old road-mender, the queer Jean Jacques
      Rousseau,
Columbus, Confucius, all to my English garden they troop,
   Under his goatskin umbrella the provident Robinson Crusoe,
And the ancestor dead long ago in Domingo or Guadaloupe.

ROBERT BRIDGES

223 *Desire*

Bright eyes, sweet lips, with many fevers fill
　　The young blood, running wildly, as it must;
　　But lips and eyes beget a strange distrust.
Electric fingers send the sudden thrill
Through senses unsubservient to the will;
　　The flames die down, and leave a dim disgust;
　　Unfragrant kisses turn to drouth and dust;
I kiss; I feast; but I am hungry still.

O woman, woman, passionate but strong!
　　True to thy love as needle to the pole—
　　　　True to the truth, and not alone to me—
O mate and friend, elusive in the throng,
　　　　With thy clear brows, thy straight and upright soul,
　　　　Nameless—unknown—my hunger is for thee!

ADA CAMBRIDGE

224 *God's Grandeur*

THE world is charged with the grandeur of God.
   It will flame out, like shining from shook foil;
   It gathers to a greatness, like the ooze of oil
Crushed. Why do men then now not reck his rod?
Generations have trod, have trod, have trod;
   And all is seared with trade; bleared, smeared with toil;
   And wears man's smudge and shares man's smell: the soil
Is bare now, nor can foot feel, being shod.

And for all this, nature is never spent;
   There lives the dearest freshness deep down things;
And though the last lights off the black West went
   Oh, morning, at the brown brink eastward, springs—
Because the Holy Ghost over the bent
   World broods with warm breast and with ah! bright wings.

GERARD MANLEY HOPKINS

225   *The Windhover:*

To Christ our Lord

❧❧❧

I CAUGHT this morning morning's minion, king-
   dom of daylight's dauphin, dapple-dawn-drawn Falcon, in
      his riding
   Of the rolling level underneath him steady air, and striding
High there, how he rung upon the rein of a wimpling wing
In his ecstasy! then off, off forth on swing,
   As a skate's heel sweeps smooth on a bow-bend: the hurl and
      gliding
   Rebuffed the big wind. My heart in hiding
Stirred for a bird,—the achieve of, the mastery of the thing!

Brute beauty and valour and act, oh, air, pride, plume here
   Buckle! AND the fire that breaks from thee then, a billion
Times told lovelier, more dangerous, O my chevalier!

   No wonder of it: shéer plód makes plough down sillion
Shine, and blue-bleak embers, ah my dear,
   Fall, gall themselves, and gash gold-vermilion.

GERARD MANLEY HOPKINS

226   *Hurrahing in Harvest*

SUMMER ends now; now, barbarous in beauty, the stooks rise
    Around; up above, what wind-walks! what lovely behaviour
    Of silk-sack clouds! has wilder, wilful-wavier
Meal-drift moulded ever and melted across skies?

I walk, I lift up, I lift up heart, eyes,
    Down all that glory in the heavens to glean our Saviour;
    And, éyes, heárt, what looks, what lips yet gave you a
Rapturous love's greeting of realer, of rounder replies?

And the azurous hung hills are his world-wielding shoulder
    Majestic—as a stallion stalwart, very-violet-sweet!—
These things, these things were here and but the beholder
    Wanting; which two when they once meet,
The heart rears wings bold and bolder
    And hurls for him, O half hurls earth for him off under his feet.

GERARD MANLEY HOPKINS

227 *Felix Randal*

FELIX RANDAL the farrier, O is he dead then? my duty all
    ended,
Who have watched his mould of man, big-boned and hardy-
    handsome
Pining, pining, till time when reason rambled in it and some
Fatal four disorders, fleshed there, all contended?

Sickness broke him. Impatient he cursed at first, but mended
Being anointed and all; though a heavenlier heart began some
Months earlier, since I had our sweet reprieve and ransom
Tendered to him. Ah well, God rest him all road ever he offended!

This seeing the sick endears them to us, us too it endears.
My tongue had taught thee comfort, touch had quenched thy
    tears,
Thy tears that touched my heart, child, Felix, poor Felix Randal;

How far from then forethought of, all thy more boisterous years,
When thou at the random grim forge, powerful amidst peers,
Didst fettle for the great grey drayhorse his bright and battering
    sandal!

GERARD MANLEY HOPKINS

228   *Spelt from Sibyl's Leaves*

❦❦❦

EARNEST, earthless, equal, attuneable, | vaulty, voluminous,
   . . . stupendous
Evening strains to be tíme's vást, | womb-of-all, home-of-all,
   hearse-of-all night.
Her fond yellow hornlight wound to the west, | her wild hollow
   hoarlight hung to the height
Waste; her earliest stars, earl-stars, | stárs principal, overbend
   us,
Fíre-féaturing heaven. For earth | her being has unbound, her
   dapple is at an end, as-
tray or aswarm, all throughther, in throngs; | self ín self steepèd
   and páshed—qúite
Disremembering, dísmémbering | áll now. Heart, you round
   me right
With: Óur évening is over us; óur night | whélms, whélms, ánd
   will end us.

Only the beak-leaved boughs dragonish | damask the tool-
   smooth bleak light; black,
Ever so black on it. Óur tale, O óur oracle! | Lét life, wáned, ah
   lét life wind

Off hér once skéined stained véined varíety | upon, áll on twó
    spools; párt, pen, páck
Now her áll in twó flocks, twó folds—black, white; | right,
    wrong; reckon but, reck but, mind
But thése two; wáre of a wórld where bút these | twó tell, each
    off the óther; of a rack
Where, selfwrung, selfstrung, sheathe-and shelterless, |
    thóughts agaínst thoughts ín groans grínd.

GERARD MANLEY HOPKINS

229 *'I wake and feel the fell of dark, not day'*

I WAKE and feel the fell of dark, not day.
What hours, O what black hoürs we have spent
This night! what sights you, heart, saw; ways you went!
And more must, in yet longer light's delay.

  With witness I speak this. But where I say
Hours I mean years, mean life. And my lament
Is cries countless, cries like dead letters sent
To dearest him that lives alas! away.

 I am gall, I am heartburn. God's most deep decree
Bitter would have me taste: my taste was me;
Bones built in me, flesh filled, blood brimmed the curse.
 Selfyeast of spirit a dull dough sours. I see
The lost are like this, and their scourge to be
As I am mine, their sweating selves; but worse.

GERARD MANLEY HOPKINS

230 *Am I to Lose You?*

'Am I to lose you now?' The words were light;
   You spoke them, hardly seeking a reply,
   That day I bid you quietly 'Good-bye,'
And sought to hide my soul away from sight.
The question echoed, dear, through many a night,—
   My question, not your own—most wistfully;
   'Am I to lose him?'—asked my heart of me;
'Am I to lose him now, and lose him quite?'

And only you can tell me. Do you care
   That sometimes we in quietness should stand
   As fellow-solitudes, hand firm in hand,
And thought with thought and hope with hope compare?
What is your answer? Mine must ever be,
   'I greatly need your friendship: leave it me.'

LOUISA SARAH BEVINGTON

231 *Ebbtide at Sundown*

O LARGER is remembrance than desire!
O deeper than all longing is regret!
The tide is gone, the sands are rippled yet;
The sun is gone: the hills are lifted higher,
Crested with rose. Ah, why should we require
Sight of the sea, the sun? The sands are wet,
And in their glassy flaws huge record set
Of the ebbed stream, the little ball of fire.
Gone, they are gone! But oh, so freshly gone,
So rich in vanishing we ask not where—
So close upon us is the bliss that shone,
And oh, so thickly it impregns the air!
Closer in beating heart we could not be
To the sunk sun, the far, surrendered sea.

MICHAEL FIELD
(KATHERINE BRADLEY AND
EDITH COOPER)

232   *The Mummy invokes his Soul*

DOWN to me quickly, down! I am such dust,
Baked, pressed together; let my flesh be fanned
With thy fresh breath: come from thy reedy land
Voiceful with birds; divert me, for I lust
To break, to crumble—prick with pores this crust!
And fall apart delicious, loosening sand.
Oh, joy, I feel thy breath, I feel thy hand
That searches for my heart, and trembles just
Where once it beat. How light thy touch, thy frame!
Surely thou perchest on the summer trees. . . .
And the garden that we loved? Soul, take thine ease,
I am content, so thou enjoy the same
Sweet terraces and founts, content, for thee,
To burn in this immense torpidity.

MICHAEL FIELD
(KATHERINE BRADLEY AND
EDITH COOPER)

233 *Maidenhair*

PLATO of the clear, dreaming eye and brave
Imaginings, conceived, withdrawn from light,
The hollow of man's heart even as a cave.
With century-slow dropping stalactite
My heart was dripping tedious in despair.
But yesterday, awhile before I slept:
I wake to find it live with maidenhair
And mosses to the spiky pendants crept.
Great prodigies there are—Jehovah's flood
Widening the margin of the Red Sea shore,—
Great marvel when the moon is turned to blood
It is to mortals, yet I marvel more
At the soft rifts, the pushings at my heart,
That lift the great stones of its rock apart.

MICHAEL FIELD
(KATHERINE BRADLEY AND
EDITH COOPER)

234   *Thoughts in Separation*

WE never meet; yet we meet day by day
  Upon those hills of life, dim and immense—
  The good we love, and sleep, our innocence.
O hills of life, high hills! And, higher than they,

Our guardian spirits meet at prayer and play.
  Beyond pain, joy, and hope, and long suspense,
  Above the summits of our souls, far hence,
An angel meets an angel on the way.

Beyond all good I ever believed of thee,
  Or thou of me, these always love and live.
And though I fail of thy ideal of me,

My angel falls not short. They greet each other.
  Who knows, they may exchange the kiss we give,
Thou to thy crucifix, I to my mother.

ALICE MEYNELL

235 *Renouncement*

I MUST not think of thee; and, tired yet strong,
　　I shun the thought that lurks in all delight—
　　The thought of thee—and in the blue Heaven's height,
And in the sweetest passage of a song.

Oh, just beyond the fairest thoughts that throng
　　This breast, the thought of thee waits, hidden yet bright;
　　But it must never, never come in sight;
I must stop short of thee the whole day long.

But when sleep comes to close each difficult day,
　　When night gives pause to the long watch I keep,
　　And all my bonds I needs must loose apart,

Must doff my will as raiment laid away,—
　　With the first dream that comes with the first sleep
　　I run, I run, I am gathered to thy heart.

ALICE MEYNELL

236 'One night I dreamt that in a gleaming hall'

ONE night I dreamt that in a gleaming hall
You played, and overhead the air was sweet
With waving kerchiefs; then a sudden fall
Of flowers; and jewels clashed about your feet.
Around you glittering forms, a starry ring,
In echo sang of youth and golden ease:
You leant to me a moment, crying—'Sing,
If, as you say, you love me, sing with these.'—
    In vain my lips were opened, for my throat
Was choked somewhere, my tongue was sore and dry,
And in my soul alone the answering note;
Till, in a piercing discord, one shrill cry,
As of a hunted creature, from me broke.
You laughed, and in great bitterness I woke.

DIGBY MACKWORTH DOLBEN

237 ## *At Queensferry*

To W. G. S.

❧❧❧❧

THE blackbird sang, the skies were clear and clean;
We bowled along a road that curved a spine
Superbly sinuous and serpentine
Through silent symphonies of summer green.
Sudden the Forth came on us—sad of mien,
No cloud to colour it, no breeze to line:
A sheet of dark, dull glass, without a sign
Of life or death, two spits of sand between.
Water and sky merged blank in mist together,
The Fort loomed spectral, and the Guardship's spars
Traced vague, black shadows on the shimmery glaze:
We felt the dim, strange years, the gray, strange weather,
The still, strange land, unvexed of sun or stars,
Where Lancelot rides clanking through the haze.

WILLIAM ERNEST HENLEY

238   *Speechless:*

Upon the marriage of two deaf and dumb persons

THEIR lips upon each other's lips are laid;
  Strong moans of joy, wild laughter, and short cries
  Seem uttered in the passion of their eyes.
He sees her body fair, and fallen head,
And she the face whereon her soul is fed;
  And by the way her white breasts sink and rise,
  He knows she must be shaken by sweet sighs;
Though all delight of sound for them be dead.

They dance a strange, weird measure, who know not
  The tune to which their dancing feet are led;
Their breath in kissing is made doubly hot
  With flame of pent-up speech; strange light is shed
    About their spirits, as they mix and meet
    In passion-lighted silence, 'tranced and sweet.

PHILIP BOURKE MARSTON

239   *'Nay, but I fancy somehow, year by year'*

NAY, but I fancy somehow, year by year
    The hard road waxing easier to my feet;
    Nay, but I fancy as the season's fleet
    I shall grow ever dearer to my dear.
Hope is so strong that it has conquered fear;
    Love follows, crowned and glad for fear's defeat.
    Down the long future I behold us, sweet,
Pass, and grow ever dearer and more near,
Pass and go onward into the mild land
    Where the blond harvests slumber all the noon,
    And the pale sky bends downward to the sea;
Pass, and go forward, ever hand in hand,
    Till all the plain be quickened with the moon,
    And the lit windows beckon o'er the lea.

ROBERT LOUIS STEVENSON

240

Santa Decca

THE Gods are dead: no longer do we bring
    To grey-eyed Pallas crowns of olive-leaves!
    Demeter's child no more hath tithe of sheaves,
And in the noon the careless shepherds sing,
For Pan is dead, and all the wantoning
    By secret glade and devious haunt is o'er:
    Young Hylas seeks the water-springs no more;
Great Pan is dead, and Mary's Son is King.

And yet—perchance in this sea-trancèd isle,
    Chewing the bitter fruit of memory,
    Some God lies hidden in the asphodel.
Ah Love! if such there be then it were well
    For us to fly his anger: nay, but see
    The leaves are stirring: let us watch a-while.

OSCAR WILDE

241   *Art and Life*

❦❦❦❦❦❦

WHEN autumn comes, my orchard trees alone
Shall bear no fruit to deck the reddening year—
    When apple gatherers climb the branches sere,
Only on mine no harvest shall be grown.
For when the pearly blossom first was blown,
    I filled my hands with delicate buds and dear,
    I dipped them in thine icy waters clear,
O well of Art! and turned them all to stone.

Therefore, when winter comes, I shall not eat
Of mellow apples such as others prize:
    I shall go hungry in a magic spring!—
All round my head and bright before mine eyes
The barren, strange, eternal blossoms meet,
    While I, not less an-hungered, gaze and sing.

AGNES MARY FRANCES ROBINSON

242 *Non Pax—Expectatio*

Hush! 'tis the gap between two lightnings. Room
Is none for peace in this thou callest peace,
This breathing-while wherein the breathings cease.
The pulses sicken, hearkening through the gloom.
Afar the thunders of a coming doom
Ramp on the cowering winds. Lo! at the dread,
Thy heart's tomb yawns and renders up its dead,—
The hopes-'gainst hope embalmèd in its womb.

Canst thou endure, if the pent flood o'erflows?
Who is estated heir to constancy?
Behold, I hardly know if I outlast
The minute underneath whose heel I lie;
Yet I endure, have stayed the minute passed,
Perchance may stay the next. Who knows, who knows?

FRANCIS THOMPSON

243 *To a Piano*

O CASKET of sweet sounds, wherein there lieth
  A sound to lull the weary man to sleep,
  A sound to make the hard and tearless weep,
A sound that every sound on earth defieth,
And only to one hand on earth replieth,
  What time her fingers varied measure keep,
  To drag it wooingly from out the deep
That, softly wooed by others, only sigheth!
If I might win me that remembered strain
  By reverent lifting of thy gleamy lid,
I could forget the sorrowful refrain
  Of all the world shall do—is doing—did.
Pandora's prisoned hope was not more vain.
  The casket's there, the melody is hid.

MARY COLERIDGE

244   *'I Shall Forget'*

ALTHOUGH my life, which thou hast scarred and shaken,
   Retains awhile some influence of thee,
As shells, by faithless waves, long since forsaken,
   Still murmur with the music of the Sea,

I shall forget. Not thine the haunting beauty,
   Which, once beheld, for ever holds the heart,
Or, if resigned from stress of fate or duty,
   Takes part of life away:—the dearer part.

I gave thee love; thou gavest but desire.
   Ah, the delusion of that summer night!
Thy soul vibrated at the rate of fire;
   Mine, with the rhythm of the waves of light.

It is my love for thee that I regret,
Not thee, thyself, and hence,—I shall forget!

LAURENCE HOPE
(ADELA FLORENCE CORY NICOLSON)

245   *The Hour of the Angel*

SOONER or late—in earnest or in jest—
  (But the stakes are no jest) Ithuriel's Hour
Will spring on us, for the first time, the test
  Of our sole unbacked competence and power
  Up to the limit of our years and dower
Of judgment—or beyond. But here we have
Prepared long since our garland or our grave.
  For, at that hour, the sum of all our past,
  Act, habit, thought, and passion, shall be cast
  In one addition, be it more or less,
  And as that reading runs so shall we do;
  Meeting, astounded, victory at the last,
  Or, first and last, our own unworthiness.
And none can change us though they die to save!

RUDYARD KIPLING

246 *At Seventeen*

You were a child, and liked me, yesterday.
To-day you are a woman, and perhaps
Those softer eyes betoken the sweet lapse
Of liking into loving: who shall say?
Only I know that there can be for us
No liking more, nor any kisses now,
But they shall wake sweet shame upon your brow
Sweetly, or in a rose calamitous.

Trembling upon the verge of some new dawn
You stand, as if awakened out of sleep,
And it is I who cried to you, 'Arise!',
I who would fain call back the child that's gone,
And what you lost for me would have you keep,
Fearing to meet the woman of your eyes.

ARTHUR SYMONS

247 *Leda and the Swan*

A SUDDEN blow: the great wings beating still
Above the staggering girl, her thighs caressed
By the dark webs, her nape caught in his bill,
He holds her helpless breast upon his breast.

How can those terrified vague fingers push
The feathered glory from her loosening thighs?
And how can body, laid in that white rush,
But feel the strange heart beating where it lies?

A shudder in the loins engenders there
The broken wall, the burning roof and tower
And Agamemnon dead.
                              Being so caught up,
So mastered by the brute blood of the air,
Did she put on his knowledge with his power
Before the indifferent beak could let her drop?

WILLIAM BUTLER YEATS

248 *Meru*

Civilisation is hooped together, brought
Under a rule, under the semblance of peace
By manifold illusion; but man's life is thought,
And he, despite his terror, cannot cease
Ravening through century after century,
Ravening, raging, and uprooting that he may come
Into the desolation of reality:
Egypt and Greece, good-bye, and good-bye, Rome!

Hermits upon Mount Meru or Everest,
Caverned in night under the drifted snow,
Or where that snow and winter's dreadful blast
Beat down upon their naked bodies, know
That day brings round the night, that before dawn
His glory and his monuments are gone.

WILLIAM BUTLER YEATS

249 *Fleming Helphenstine*

AT first I thought there was a superfine
Persuasion in his face; but the free glow
That filled it when he stopped and cried, 'Hollo!'
Shone joyously, and so I let it shine.
He said his name was Fleming Helphenstine,
But be that as it may;—I only know
He talked of this and that and So-and-So,
And laughed and chaffed like any friend of mine.

But soon, with a queer, quick frown, he looked at me,
And I looked hard at him; and there we gazed
In a strained way that made us cringe and wince:
Then, with a wordless clogged apology
That sounded half confused and half amazed,
He dodged,—and I have never seen him since.

EDWIN ARLINGTON ROBINSON

250   *Lingard and the Stars*

THE table hurled itself, to our surprise,
At Lingard, and anon rapped eagerly:
'When earth is cold and there is no more sea,
There will be what was Lingard. Otherwise,
Why lure the race to ruin through the skies?
And why have Leffingwell, or Calverly?' —
'I wish the ghost would give his name,' said he;
And searching gratitude was in his eyes.

He stood then by the window for a time,
And only after the last midnight chime
Smote the day dead did he say anything:
'Come out, my little one, the stars are bright;
Come out, you lælaps, and inhale the night.'
And so he went away with Clavering.

EDWIN ARLINGTON ROBINSON

Why he was There

251

❧❧❧❧❧❧

MUCH as he left it when he went from us
Here was the room again where he had been
So long that something of him should be seen,
Or felt—and so it was. Incredulous,
I turned about, loath to be greeted thus,
And there he was in his old chair, serene
As ever, and as laconic and as lean
As when he lived, and as cadaverous.

Calm as he was of old when we were young,
He sat there gazing at the pallid flame
Before him. 'And how far will this go on?'
I thought. He felt the failure of my tongue,
And smiled: 'I was not here until you came;
And I shall not be here when you are gone.'

EDWIN ARLINGTON ROBINSON

252 *Design*

I FOUND a dimpled spider, fat and white,
On a white heal-all, holding up a moth
Like a white piece of rigid satin cloth—
Assorted characters of death and blight
Mixed ready to begin the morning right,
Like the ingredients of a witches' broth—
A snow-drop spider, a flower like a froth,
And dead wings carried like a paper kite.

What had that flower to do with being white,
The wayside blue and innocent heal-all?
What brought the kindred spider to that height,
Then steered the white moth thither in the night?
What but design of darkness to appall?—
If design govern in a thing so small.

ROBERT FROST

253 *The Silken Tent*

S H E is as in a field a silken tent
At midday when a sunny summer breeze
Has dried the dew and all its ropes relent,
So that in guys it gently sways at ease,
And its supporting central cedar pole,
That is its pinnacle to heavenward
And signifies the sureness of the soul,
Seems to owe naught to any single cord,
But strictly held by none, is loosely bound
By countless silken ties of love and thought
To everything on earth the compass round,
And only by one's going slightly taut
In the capriciousness of summer air
Is of the slightest bondage made aware.

ROBERT FROST

254 *Meeting and Passing*

As I went down the hill along the wall
There was a gate I had leaned at for the view
And had just turned from when I first saw you
As you came up the hill. We met. But all
We did that day was mingle great and small
Footprints in summer dust as if we drew
The figure of our being less than two
But more than one as yet. Your parasol
Pointed the decimal off with one deep thrust.
And all the time we talked you seemed to see
Something down there to smile at in the dust.
(Oh, it was without prejudice to me!)
Afterward I went past what you had passed
Before we met and you what I had passed.

ROBERT FROST

255 *'Some eyes condemn the earth*
they gaze upon'

SOME eyes condemn the earth they gaze upon:
Some wait patiently till they know far more
Than earth can tell them: some laugh at the whole
As folly of another's making: one
I knew that laughed because he saw, from core
To rind, not one thing worth the laugh his soul
Had ready at waking: some eyes have begun
With laughing; some stand startled at the door.

Others, too, I have seen rest, question, roll,
Dance, shoot. And many I have loved watching. Some
I could not take my eyes from till they turned
And loving died. I had not found my goal.
But thinking of your eyes, dear, I become
Dumb: for they flamed, and it was me they burned.

EDWARD THOMAS

256 *Glory of Women*

You love us when we're heroes, home on leave,
Or wounded in a mentionable place.
You worship decorations; you believe
That chivalry redeems the war's disgrace.
You make us shells. You listen with delight,
By tales of dirt and danger fondly thrilled.
You crown our distant ardours while we fight,
And mourn our laurelled memories when we're killed.
You can't believe that British troops 'retire'
When hell's last horror breaks them, and they run,
Trampling the terrible corpses—blind with blood.
   O German mother dreaming by the fire,
     While you are knitting socks to send your son
     His face is trodden deeper in the mud.

SIEGFRIED SASSOON

257   *Sporting Acquaintances*

I WATCHED old squatting Chimpanzee: he traced
His painful patterns in the dirt: I saw
Red-haired Ourang-Utang, whimsical-faced,
Chewing a sportsman's meditative straw.
I'd known them years ago, and half-forgotten
They'd come to grief. (But how, I'd never heard,
Poor beggars!) Still, it seemed so rude and rotten
To stand and gape at them with never a word.

I ventured 'Ages since we met,' and tried
My candid smile of friendship. No success.
One scratched his hairy thigh, while t'other sighed
And glanced away. I saw they liked me less
Than when, on Epsom Downs, in cloudless weather,
We backed The Tetrarch and got drunk together.

SIEGFRIED SASSOON

258 *The Hill*

BREATHLESS, we flung us on the windy hill,
　　Laughed in the sun, and kissed the lovely grass.
　　You said, 'Through glory and ecstasy we pass;
Wind, sun, and earth remain, the birds sing still,
When we are old, are old. . . .' 'And when we die
　　All's over that is ours; and life burns on
Through other lovers, other lips,' said I,
　　'Heart of my heart, our heaven is now, is won!'

'We are Earth's best, that learnt her lesson here.
　　Life is our cry. We have kept the faith!' we said;
　　'We shall go down with unreluctant tread
Rose-crowned into the darkness!' . . . Proud we were,
And laughed, that had such brave true things to say.
—And then you suddenly cried, and turned away.

RUPERT BROOKE

259 *Sonnet Reversed*

❧❧❧

HAND trembling towards hand; the amazing lights
Of heart and eye. They stood on supreme heights.

Ah, the delirious weeks of honeymoon!
  Soon they returned, and, after strange adventures,
Settled at Balham by the end of June.
  Their money was in Can. Pacs. B. Debentures,
And in Antofagastas. Still he went
  Cityward daily; still she did abide
At home. And both were really quite content
  With work and social pleasures. Then they died.
They left three children (besides George, who drank):
  The eldest Jane, who married Mr Bell,
William, the head-clerk in the County Bank,
  And Henry, a stock-broker, doing well.

RUPERT BROOKE

260 *'Children of wealth in your warm nursery'*

CHILDREN of wealth in your warm nursery,
Set in the cushioned window-seat to watch
The volleying snow, guarded invisibly
By the clear double pane through which no touch
Untimely penetrates, you cannot tell
What winter means; its cruel truths to you
Are only sound and sight; your citadel
Is safe from feeling, and from knowledge too.

Go down, go out to elemental wrong,
Waste your too round limbs, tan your skin too white;
The glass of comfort, ignorance, seems strong
To-day, and yet perhaps this very night

You'll wake to horror's wrecking fire—your home
Is wired within for this, in every room.

ELIZABETH DARYUSH

261 *Where I?*

✦✦✦

THIS woman cannot live more than one year.
Her growing death is hidden in a hopeless place,
Her death is like a child growing in her,
And she knows it, you see it shine in her face.
She looks at her own hands and thinks 'In a year
These will be burnt like rags in the crematory.
I shall not feel it. Where I? Where I? Not anywhere.'
It is strange, it gives to her face a kind of glory.
Her mind used to be lazy and heavy her face,
Now she talks all in haste, looks young and lean
And eager, her eyes glitter with eagerness,
As if she were newly born and had never seen
The beauty of things, the terror, pain, joy, the song.
—Or is it better to live at ease, dully and long?

ROBINSON JEFFERS

262 *Milton*

MILTON, his face set fair for Paradise,
And knowing that he and Paradise were lost
In separate desolation, bravely crossed
Into his second night and paid his price.
There towards the end he to the dark tower came
Set square in the gate, a mass of blackened stone
Crowned with vermilion fiends like streamers blown
From a great funnel filled with roaring flame.

Shut in his darkness, these he could not see,
But heard the steely clamour known too well
On Saturday nights in every street in Hell.
Where, past the devilish din, could Paradise be?
A footstep more, and his unblinded eyes
Saw far and near the fields of Paradise.

EDWIN MUIR

263 *The Tall Girl*

THE Queens of Hell had lissome necks to crane
At the tall girl approaching with long tread
And, when she was caught up even with them, nodded:
'If the young miss with gold hair might not disdain,
We would esteem her company over the plain,
To profit us all where the dogs will be out barking,
And we'll go by the windows where the young men are working
And tomorrow we will all come home again.'

But the Queen of Heaven on the other side of the road
In the likeness, I hear, of a plain motherly woman
Made a wry face, despite it was so common
To be worsted by the smooth ladies of Hell,
And crisped her sweet tongue: 'This never will come to good!
Just an old woman, my pet, that wishes you well.'

JOHN CROWE RANSOM

264   *Good Ships*

FLEET ships encountering on the high seas
Who speak, and then unto the vast diverge,
Two hailed each other, poised on the loud surge
Of one of Mrs. Grundy's Tuesday teas,
Nor trimmed one sail to baffle the driving breeze.
A macaroon absorbed all her emotion;
His hue was ruddy but an effect of ocean;
They exchanged the nautical technicalities.

It was only a nothing or so until they parted.
Away they went, most certainly bound for port,
So seaworthy one felt they could not sink;
Still there was a tremor shook them, I should think,
Beautiful timbers fit for storm and sport
And unto miserly merchant hulks converted.

JOHN CROWE RANSOM

265   *'The silver herring throbbed thick
in my seine'*

THE silver herring throbbed thick in my seine,
silver of life, life's silver sheen of glory;
my hands, cut with the cold, hurt with the pain
of hauling the net, pulled the heavy dory,
heavy with life, low in the water, deep
plunged to the gunwale's lips in the stress of rowing,
the pulse of rowing that puts the world to sleep,
world within world endlessly ebbing, flowing.

At length you stood on the landing and you cried,
with quick low cries you timed me stroke on stroke
as I steadily won my way with the fulling tide
and crossed the threshold where the last wave broke
and coasted over the step of water and threw
straight through the air my mooring line to you.

KENNETH LESLIE

266   *The End of the World*

QUITE unexpectedly as Vasserot
The armless ambidextrian was lighting
A match between his great and second toe
And Ralph the lion was engaged in biting
The neck of Madame Sossman while the drum
Pointed, and Teeny was about to cough
In waltz-time swinging Jocko by the thumb—
Quite unexpectedly the top blew off:

And there, there overhead, there, there, hung over
Those thousands of white faces, those dazed eyes,
There in the starless dark the poise, the hover,
There with vast wings across the canceled skies,
There in the sudden blackness the black pall
Of nothing, nothing, nothing—nothing at all.

ARCHIBALD MACLEISH

267 *'Time does not bring relief;*
you all have lied'

TIME does not bring relief; you all have lied
Who told me time would ease me of my pain!
I miss him in the weeping of the rain;
I want him at the shrinking of the tide;
The old snows melt from every mountain-side,
And last year's leaves are smoke in every lane;
But last year's bitter loving must remain
Heaped on my heart, and my old thoughts abide.
There are a hundred places where I fear
To go, — so with his memory they brim.
And entering with relief some quiet place
Where never fell his foot or shone his face
I say, 'There is no memory of him here!'
And so stand stricken, so remembering him.

EDNA ST VINCENT MILLAY

268 *'Grow not too high, grow not too far
from home'*

Grow not too high, grow not too far from home,
Green tree, whose roots are in the granite's face!
Taller than silver spire or golden dome
A tree may grow above its earthy place,
And taller than a cloud, but not so tall
The root may not be mother to the stem,
Lifting rich plenty, though the rivers fall,
To the cold sunny leaves to nourish them.
Have done with blossoms for a time, be bare;
Split rock; plunge downward; take heroic soil,—
Deeper than bones, no pasture for you there;
Deeper than water, deeper than gold and oil:
Earth's fiery core alone can feed the bough
That blooms between Orion and the Plough.

EDNA ST VINCENT MILLAY

269   *'Night is my sister, and how deep in love'*

NIGHT is my sister, and how deep in love,
How drowned in love and weedily washed ashore,
There to be fretted by the drag and shove
At the tide's edge, I lie—these things and more:
Whose arm alone between me and the sand,
Whose voice alone, whose pitiful breath brought near,
Could thaw these nostrils and unlock this hand,
She could advise you, should you care to hear.
Small chance, however, in a storm so black,
A man will leave his friendly fire and snug
For a drowned woman's sake, and bring her back
To drip and scatter shells upon the rug.
No one but Night, with tears on her dark face,
Watches beside me in this windy place.

EDNA ST VINCENT MILLAY

270 *To——*

THREE rompers run together, hand in hand.
The middle boy stops short, the others hurtle:
What bumps, what shrieks, what laughter turning turtle.
Love, racing between us two, has planned
A sudden mischief: shortly he will stand
And we shall shock. We cannot help but fall;
What matter? Why, it will not hurt at all,
Our youth is supple, and the world is sand.

Better my lips should bruise you so, than He,
Rude love, out-run our breath; you pant, and I,
I cannot run much farther; mind that we
Both laugh with love; and having tumbled, try
To go forever children, hand in hand.
The sea is rising . . . and the world is sand.

WILFRED OWEN

271 *Maundy Thursday*

BETWEEN the brown hands of a server-lad
The silver cross was offered to be kissed.
The men came up, lugubrious, but not sad,
And knelt reluctantly, half-prejudiced.
(And kissing, kissed the emblem of a creed.)
Then mourning women knelt; meek mouths they had.
(And kissed the Body of the Christ indeed.)
Young children came, with eager lips and glad.
(These kissed a silver doll, immensely bright.)
Then I, too, knelt before the acolyte.
Above the crucifix I bent my head:
The Christ was thin, and cold, and very dead:
And yet I bowed, yea, kissed—my lips did cling
(I kissed the warm live hand that held the thing.)

WILFRED OWEN

272   *'To no believable blue I turn my eyes'*

To no believable blue I turn my eyes,
Blinded with sapphire, watchet, gentian,
Shadow on snow, Mediterranean,
Midsummer or midwinter-moonlight skies.
Unstained by sight, unravished by surmise,
And uttering into the void her ban,
Her boast, her being—*I know not a man!*
Out of all thought the virgin colour flies.

After her, soul! Have in unhaving, peace,
Let thy lacklight lighten upon thee, read
So well thy sentence that it spells release.
Explore thy chain, importune suns to cede
News of thy dark—joyed with thy doom's increase,
And only by distinction of fetters freed.

SYLVIA TOWNSEND WARNER

273 *Armour*

CRABS in their shells, because they cannot play
Don Juan or the flageolet, are safe;
And every stout Sir Roger, stout Sir Ralph,
Every Black Prince, Bayard and Bourchier may
(Their ribs and rumps hermetically canned)
Securely laugh at arrow, sword and mace.
But in their polished and annealed embrace,
Beneath their iron kiss and iron hand,
The soft defenceless lips and flowery breast,
The tender, tender belly of love receive
From helm and clasping cop and urgent greave
So deep a bruise that, mortally possessed,
Love dies. Only the vulnerable will
Holds what it takes and, holding, does not kill.

ALDOUS HUXLEY

274   *The Troll's Nosegay*

A SIMPLE nosegay! was that much to ask?
(Winter still nagged, with scarce a bud yet showing.)
He loved her ill, if he resigned the task.
'Somewhere,' she cried, 'there must be blossom blowing.'
It seems my lady wept and the troll swore
By Heaven he hated tears: he'd cure her spleen—
Where she had begged one flower he'd shower fourscore,
A bunch fit to amaze a China Queen.
Cold fog-drawn Lily, pale mist-magic Rose
He conjured, and in a glassy cauldron set
With elvish unsubstantial Mignonette
And such vague bloom as wandering dreams enclose.
But she?

        Awed,

                Charmed to tears,

                        Distracted,

                                Yet—

Even yet, perhaps, a trifle piqued—who knows?

ROBERT GRAVES

275 *'When you see millions of the mouthless dead'*

❦❦❦❦

WHEN you see millions of the mouthless dead
Across your dreams in pale battalions go,
Say not soft things as other men have said,
That you'll remember. For you need not so.
Given them not praise. For, deaf, how should they know
It is not curses heaped on each gashed head?
Nor tears. Their blind eyes see not your tears flow.
Nor honour. It is easy to be dead.
Say only this, 'They are dead.' Then add thereto,
'Yet many a better one has died before.'
Then, scanning all the o'ercrowded mass, should you
Perceive one face that you loved heretofore,
It is a spook. None wears the face you knew.
Great death has made all his for evermore.

CHARLES HAMILTON SORLEY

276   *Moon-talk*

GREEN-BODIED, with small eyes of crimson fire,
By furry limb and sinuous tail they swung
From branch to branch. He chattered with desire
Beneath the frail bough where she coyly clung,
Damp with excitement. And beyond her brain
Far-throbbing peals by those strange sounds were rung
Until her lips quivered with cries like pain,
And in her eyes the Moon's white blossom hung.

I met one burning-eyed to-night, whose flesh
Was vibrant with her spirit. But I heard
Echo in each love-phrase and lofty word
The gibberings of those long-tailed ghosts of ours;
And saw the Moon break through her leafy mesh
And in the girl's eyes float like water-flowers.

EDGELL RICKWORD

277

The Zebras

To Chips Rafferty

FROM the dark woods that breathe of fallen showers,
Harnessed with level rays in golden reins,
The zebras draw the dawn across the plains
Wading knee-deep among the scarlet flowers.
The sunlight, zithering their flanks with fire,
Flashes between the shadows as they pass
Barred with electric tremors through the grass
Like wind along the gold strings of a lyre.

Into the flushed air snorting rosy plumes
That smoulder round their feet in drifting fumes,
With dove-like voices call the distant fillies,
While round the herds the stallion wheels his flight,
Engine of beauty volted with delight,
To roll his mare among the trampled lilies.

ROY CAMPBELL

278 *Full Orchestra*

My words are the poor footmen of your pride,
Of what you cry, you trumpets, each to each
With mouths of air; my speech is the dog-speech
Of yours, the Roman tongue—but mine is tied
By harsher bridles, dumb with breath and bone.
Vainly it mocks the dingo strings, the stops,
The pear-tree flying in the flute, with drops
Of music, quenched and scattered by your own.

So serving-men, who run all night with wine,
And whet their ears, and crouch upon the floor,
Sigh broken words no man has heard before
Or since, but ravished in the candleshine,
Between the push and shutting of a door,
From the great table where their masters dine.

KENNETH SLESSOR

279 *The Odor of a Metal is not Strong*

AND it will not affect your nostrils long,
But you can smell it if you let yourself,
Take nails, a fistful, from a hardware shelf,
And you can smell the iron that is in
Them—zinc wire smells, sheet-copper, tin,
And other metal objects, odorous,
Tell of their kinship to human dust:

For what are men but blood, and what is blood
But atom-iron? Blood's red, iron-rust
Is red, this patent kinship wondrous
Is told by natural ways, is even told
By fishes, distant relatives under seas
With greenish blood, in which raw manganese
Supplants warm iron, for it runs so cold.

MERRILL MOORE

280   *Inniskeen Road: July Evening*

THE bicycles go by in twos and threes—
There's a dance in Billy Brennan's barn to-night,
And there's the half-talk code of mysteries
And the wink-and-elbow language of delight.
Half-past eight and there is not a spot
Upon a mile of road, no shadow thrown
That might turn out a man or woman, not
A footfall tapping secrecies of stone.

I have what every poet hates in spite
Of all the solemn talk of contemplation.
Oh, Alexander Selkirk knew the plight
Of being king and government and nation.
A road, a mile of kingdom, I am king
Of banks and stones and every blooming thing.

PATRICK KAVANAGH

281

Epic

I HAVE lived in important places, times
When great events were decided, who owned
That half a rood of rock, a no-man's land
Surrounded by our pitchfork-armed claims.
I heard the Duffys shouting 'Damn your soul'
And old McCabe stripped to the waist, seen
Step the plot defying blue cast-steel—
'Here is the march along these iron stones'
That was the year of the Munich bother. Which
Was most important? I inclined
To lose my faith in Ballyrush and Gortin
Till Homer's ghost came whispering to my mind
He said: I made the Iliad from such
A local row. Gods make their own importance.

PATRICK KAVANAGH

282   *Fight with a Water-Spirit*

THOUGH many men had passed the ford, not one
Had ever seen that jeering water-ghost
Denying their true conquest of the stream.
But I, who saw him smile behind a stone,
Stopped, challenged him to justify his boast.
Then came the fight, exhausting as a dream,
With stuff not quite impalpable. He sank,
Sighing, at last, in a small shrinking pile.
But my victorious paean change to fright
To see once more the pale curve of his flank
There in the water, and his endless smile
Broaden behind the stone. No use to fight.
Better to give the place a holy name,
Go on with less ambition than I came.

283 *The Unfinished Race*

No runner clears the final fence,
The laurels have long since gone stale.
They must be a cardboard pretence,
These watchers crowded on the rail.

For why should crowds stay watching so
To see a race that has no end?
How many centuries ago
The runners came up round the bend.

Always they balk at this last leap,
And then recoil to try once more.
From pride or custom still they keep
On striving—those once at the fore

Distinguished only from the ruck
By their impressive long run back.

NORMAN CAMERON

284 *The Ants*

WE tunnel through your noonday out to you.
We carry our tube's narrow darkness there
Where, nostrum-plastered, with prepared air,
With old men running and trains whining through

We ants may tap your aphides for your dew.
You may not wish their sucking or our care;
Our all-but freedom, too, your branch must bear,
High as roots' depth in earth, all earth to view.

No, by too much this station the air nears.
How small a chink lets in how dire a foe.
What though the garden in one glance appears?

Winter will come and all her leaves will go.
We do not know what skeleton endures.
Carry at least her parasites below.

WILLIAM EMPSON

285   *The Sphinx*

DID it once issue from the carver's hand
Healthy? Even the earliest conquerors saw
The face of a sick ape, a bandaged paw,
A Presence in the hot invaded land.

The lion of a tortured stubborn star,
It does not like the young, nor love, nor learning:
Time hurt it like a person; it lies, turning
A vast behind on shrill America,

And witnesses. The huge hurt face accuses,
And pardons nothing, least of all success.
The answers that it utters have no uses

To those who face akimbo its distress:
'Do people like me?' No. The slave amuses
The lion: 'Am I to suffer always?' Yes.

WYSTAN HUGH AUDEN

286   *'Here war is simple like a monument'*

HERE war is simple like a monument:
A telephone is speaking to a man;
Flags on a map assert that troops were sent;
A boy brings milk in bowls. There is a plan

For living men in terror of their lives,
Who thirst at nine who were to thirst at noon,
And can be lost and are, and miss their wives,
And, unlike an idea, can die too soon.

But ideas can be true although men die,
And we can watch a thousand faces
Made active by one lie:

And maps can really point to places
Where life is evil now:
Nanking; Dachau.

WYSTAN HUGH AUDEN

287   *Edward Lear*

LEFT by his friend to breakfast alone on the white
Italian shore, his Terrible Demon arose
Over his shoulder; he wept to himself in the night,
A dirty landscape-painter who hated his nose.

The legions of cruel inquisitive They
Were so many and big like dogs: he was upset
By Germans and boats; affection was miles away:
But guided by tears he successfully reached his Regret.

How prodigious the welcome was. Flowers took his hat
And bore him off to introduce him to the tongs;
The demon's false nose made the table laugh; a cat
Soon had him waltzing madly, let him squeeze her hand;
Words pushed him to the piano to sing comic songs;

And children swarmed to him like settlers. He became a land.

                              WYSTAN HUGH AUDEN

288   *Paradise Saved*
    (another version of the Fall)

ADAM, indignant, would not eat with Eve,
They say, and she was driven from his side.
Watching the gates close on her tears, his pride
Upheld him, though he could not help but grieve

And climbed the wall, because his loneliness
Pined for her lonely figure in the dust:
Lo, there were two! God who is more than just
Sent her a helpmeet in that wilderness.

Day after day he watched them in the waste
Grow old, breaking the harsh unfriendly ground,
Bearing their children, till at last they died;
While Adam, whose fellow God had not replaced,
Lived on immortal, young, with virtue crowned,
Sterile and impotent and justified.

ALEC DERWENT HOPE

289   *'Look! The air shudders when you breathe it in'*

LOOK! The air shudders when you breathe it in.
Never in its cold flight from north to south,
Over hill's height, field's reach, lake's languid skin,
Was such warm substance as your waiting mouth.
The high noon sun clangs in your eyes, a yell
Of purest yellowness. My blue eyes catch
In yours the sound of seeing like a bell.
Your body burns the daylight like a match.

Looking at you, common sense is senseless.
The natural truth of touching is a lie
When hands view visions. Each sense is defenseless
When love deranges simple time so we
Live only in the quick eternity
Between the breathed-in air and breathed-out cry.

PAUL ENGLE

290   *About Ice*

         (A story told by a Canadian fisherman)

When you speak about ice, do you mean live ice
Which is blue, or dead ice, white as chalk?
The blue will hold the mountain in its vice,
Crawl up it, swelling, sing down at a walk.
But white is dead so cannot climb at all
And lies in valleys where it sings no more.
One island held that not unusual,
Familiar with white along her shore,
Thinking all ice lay thus, motionless, dead,
The blue ice came and calmly ravished her
Of all her beauty of trees and moss, bled
Her lichen to the rock, leaving her bare
As that door. Stone was that island's surplice,
Who thought ice meant merely her kind of ice.

                              MALCOLM LOWRY

291 *Your Absence*

DURING your absence, when I swept the floor—
A long grey hair among the household dust.
An empty room, two petals by the door—
Relics of what mankind appears to trust
When flesh is failing, though nature equally
With art needs human health to keep its place
In human consciousness. Catastrophe
Shows more of its veiled but ever haunting face.

Darwinian miracle, that now has gone
Somewhat amiss, I see is not mine but yours
Alone to go on holding, or to lose;
Although when I receive at length the news
That you're to live I find another cause
For living, and realise I needed one.

ROY FULLER

292 *To My Mother*

Most near, most dear, most loved and most far,
Under the window where I often found her
Sitting as huge as Asia, seismic with laughter,
Gin and chicken helpless in her Irish hand,
Irresistible as Rabelais, but most tender for
The lame dogs and hurt birds that surround her,—
She is a procession no one can follow after
But be like a little dog following a brass band.

She will not glance up at the bomber, or condescend
To drop her gin and scuttle to a cellar,
But lean on the mahogany table like a mountain
Whom only faith can move, and so I send
O all my faith, and all my love to tell her
That she will move from mourning into morning.

GEORGE BARKER

293

For my Daughter

❀❀❀❀❀❀

LOOKING into my daughter's eyes I read
Beneath the innocence of morning flesh
Concealed, hintings of death she does not heed.
Coldest of winds have blown this hair, and mesh
Of seaweed snarled these miniatures of hands;
The night's slow poison, tolerant and bland,
Has moved her blood. Parched years that I have seen
That may be hers appear: foul, lingering
Death in certain war, the slim legs green.
Or, fed on hate, she relishes the sting
Of others' agony; perhaps the cruel
Bride of a syphilitic or a fool.
These speculations sour in the sun.
I have no daughter. I desire none.

WELDON KEES

294 *Among those Killed in the Dawn Raid was a Man Aged a Hundred*

❦❦❦

WHEN the morning was waking over the war
He put on his clothes and stepped out and he died,
The locks yawned loose and a blast blew them wide,
He dropped where he loved on the burst pavement stone
And the funeral grains of the slaughtered floor.
Tell his street on its back he stopped a sun
And the craters of his eyes grew springshoots and fire
When all the keys shot from the locks, and rang.
Dig no more for the chains of his grey-haired heart.
The heavenly ambulance drawn by a wound
Assembling waits for the spade's ring on the cage.
O keep his bones away from that common cart,
The morning is flying on the wings of his age
And a hundred storks perch on the sun's right hand.

DYLAN THOMAS

295 *The Last Things*

OF course there's always a last everything.
The last meal, the last drink, the last sex.
The last meeting with a friend. The last
stroking of the last cat, the last
sight of a son or daughter. Some would be more
charged with emotion than others—if one knew.
It's not knowing that makes it all so piquant.
A good many lasts have taken place already.

Then there are last words, variously reported,
such as: Don't let poor Nelly starve. Or:
I think I could eat one of Bellamy's veal pies.
If there were time I'd incline to a summary:
Alcohol made my life shorter but more interesting.
My father said (not last perhaps): Say goodbye to Gavin.

GAVIN EWART

296 *I am the Great Sun*

From a Normandy crucifix of 1632

I AM the great sun, but you do not see me,
  I am your husband, but you turn away.
I am the captive, but you do not free me,
  I am the captain you will not obey.

I am the truth, but you will not believe me,
  I am the city where you will not stay,
I am your wife, your child, but you will leave me,
  I am that God to whom you will not pray.

I am your counsel, but you do not hear me,
  I am the lover whom you will betray,
I am the victor, but you do not cheer me,
  I am the holy dove whom you will slay.

I am your life, but if you will not name me,
Seal up your soul with tears, and never blame me.

CHARLES CAUSLEY

297   *Inauguration Day: January 1953*

THE snow had buried Stuyvesant.
The subways drummed the vaults. I heard
the El's green girders charge on Third,
Manhattan's truss of adamant,
that groaned in ermine, slummed on want. . . .
Cyclonic zero of the Word,
God of our armies, who interred
Cold Harbor's blue immortals, Grant!
Horseman, your sword is in the groove!
Ice, ice. Our wheels no longer move;
Look, the fixed stars, all just alike
as lack-land atoms, split apart,
and the Republic summons Ike,
the mausoleum in her heart.

ROBERT LOWELL

298   *Watching Tennis*

LIGHT, in light breezes and a favouring sun,
You moved, like a dancer, to the glancing ball,
And the dance and the game seemed one
To me, unmarked spectator by the wall—

Always spectator, nor apt at any sport—
And you free burgess of the summer air;
Embraced within the Iron Maiden, Thought,
I of my body's poverty am aware.

How could I guess that all-consoling night,
Confider and concealer of secrets, should conduct
You to lie easy in my fumbling arms?

Yet, by the chances of the game betrayed,
Your mouth on mine found out its silent need,
And my discordant nerves peace in your limbs.

JOHN HEATH-STUBBS

299   *The Illiterate*

Touching your goodness, I am like a man
Who turns a letter over in his hand
And you might think this was because the hand
Was unfamiliar but, truth is, the man
Has never had a letter from anyone;
And now he is both afraid of what it means
And ashamed because he has no other means
To find out what it says than to ask someone.

His uncle could have left the farm to him,
Or his parents died before he sent them word,
Or the dark girl changed and want him for beloved.
Afraid and letter-proud, he keeps it with him.
What would you call his feeling for the words
That keep him rich and orphaned and beloved?

WILLIAM MEREDITH

300   *'A shilpit dog fucks grimly by the close'*

A SHILPIT dog fucks grimly by the close.
Late shadows lengthen slowly, slogans fade.
The YY PARTICK TOI grins from its shade
like the last strains of some lost *libera nos
a malo*. No deliverer ever rose
from these stone tombs to get the hell they made
unmade. The same weans never made the grade.
The same grey street sends back the ball it throws.
Under the darkness of a twisted pram
a cat's eyes glitter. Glittering stars press
between the silent chimney-cowls and cram
the higher spaces with their SOS.
Don't shine a torch on the ragwoman's dram.
Coats keep the evil cold out less and less.

EDWIN MORGAN

301   *'The winter deepening, the hay all in'*

THE winter deepening, the hay all in,
The barn fat with cattle, the apple-crop
Conveyed to market or the fragrant bin,
He thinks the time has come to make a stop,

And sinks half-grudging in his firelit seat,
Though with his heavy body's full consent,
In what would be the posture of defeat,
But for that look of rigorous content.

Outside, the night dives down like one great crow
Against his cast-off clothing where it stands
Up to the knees in miles of hustled snow,

Flapping and jumping like a kind of fire,
And floating skyward its abandoned hands
In gestures of invincible desire.

RICHARD WILBUR

302   *Jacob's Ladder*

IT was agreed we would not mount by those
Platonic ladders planted on the heart,
Minds that abide the body and its throes,
Reluctantly, and only for a start.
But Jacob's is a ladder we ascend
Without our knowing any sense of strain,
To upland air that we need not expend
One gulp of carnal breathing to attain.
So here we are upon the heights, my love,
Although in habit's level pastures still.
We want, and yet we do not want, the skill
To scale the peaks that others tell us of,
Where breathing gets so difficult, and the will
Kicks back the ground it tries to rise above.

DONALD DAVIE

303 *Whatever Happened?*

AT once whatever happened starts receding.
Panting, and back on board, we line the rail
With trousers ripped, light wallets, and lips bleeding.

Yes, gone, thank God! Remembering each detail
We toss for half the night, but find next day
All's kodak-distant. Easily, then (though pale),

'Perspective brings significance,' we say,
Unhooding our photometers, and, snap!
What can't be printed can be thrown away.

Later, it's just a latitude: the map
Points out how unavoidable it was:
'Such coastal bedding always means mishap.'

Curses? The dark? Struggling? Where's the source
Of these yarns now (except in nightmares, of course)?

PHILIP LARKIN

304 *Summer Storm*

In that so sudden summer storm they tried
Each bed, couch, closet, carpet, car-seat, table,
Both river banks, five fields, a mountain side,
Covering as much ground as they were able.

A lady, coming on them in the dark
In a white fixture, wrote to the newspapers
Complaining of the statues in the park.
By Cupid, but they cut some pretty capers!

The envious oxen in still rings would stand
Ruminating. Their sweet incessant plows
I think had changed the contours of the land
And made two modest conies move their house.

God rest them well, and firmly shut the door.
Now they are married Nature breathes once more.

LOUIS SIMPSON

305 *The Midnight Snack*

WHEN I was little and he was riled
It never entered my father's head
Not to flare up, roar and turn red.
Mother kept cool and smiled.

Now every night I tiptoe straight
Through my darkened kitchen for
The refrigerator door—
It opens, the inviolate!

Illumined as in dreams I take
A glass of milk, a piece of cake,
Then stealthily retire,

Mindful of how the gas stove's black-
Browed pilot eye's blue fire
Burns into my turned back.

JAMES MERRILL

306 *Beehive Cell*

THERE'S no comfort inside me, only a small
Hart's-tongue sprouting square, with pyramidal headroom
For one man alone kneeling down: a smell
Of peregrine mutes and eremitical boredom.

Once, in my thirteen hundred years on this barren
Island, have I felt a woman giving birth,
On her own in my spinal cerebellic souterrain,
To a living child, as she knelt on earth.

She crawled under my lintel that purgatorial night
Her menfolk marooned her out of their coracle
To pick dillisk and sloke. What hand brought a light
With angelica root for the pain of her miracle?

Three days she throve in me, suckling the child,
Doing all she had to do, the sea going wild.

RICHARD MURPHY

307 *'It's there, somewhere in the Platonic cold store'*

IT's there, somewhere in the Platonic cold store,
the work of art all computers love,
very Greek, very rational, yet so much more—
a Mahlerian *Abmarsch* perfected from above.

And the perfection floats in professors' hair,
ends up as a well-displayed and priceless junk:
the luckier art is remade in the air,
holy bubbles mark where Schönberg sunk.

A page is turned—eureka, a snatch of tune
is playing itself, the piss-proud syllables
are unveiling a difficult prosody,

two unclean bodies are seeking pleasure—the moon
goes into Alcaics; at six bells
Agamemnon comes into the bathroom to die.

PETER PORTER

308   *Freedom*

THROUGH the vast crowded wards, thousands came round.
Limbs twitched; mouths opened, uttering strange old cries;
Wild smiles and tears, and snarls at what went on
Through decades of paralysis.
                              Bodies are found
Strewn in the corridors. A doctor lies
Battered in blood. The warders have all gone,
Savaged by patients who woke up to see
The doors were open. Healers are unmasked
As torturers; nurses crucified
When drugs, withdrawn, reveal them all to be
Captors and guards.
                              And those who this way died
Are faceless as their patients.
                                        And some asked
How the great hospital would care for those
Who lie there still, free, in a deep repose.

ANTHONY THWAITE

309 *Le Loupgarou*

A CURIOUS tale that threaded through the town
Through greying women sewing under eaves,
Was how his greed had brought old Le Brun down,
Greeted by slowly shutting jalousies
When he approached them in white-linen suit,
Pink glasses, cork hat, and tap-tapping cane,
A dying man licensed to sell sick fruit,
Ruined by fiends with whom he'd made a bargain.
It seems one night, these Christian witches said,
He changed himself to an Alsatian hound,
A slavering lycanthrope hot on a scent,
But his own watchman dealt the thing a wound
Which howled and lugged its entrails, trailing wet
With blood back to its doorstep, almost dead.

DEREK WALCOTT

310   *Looking at Her*

WHEN he looked at her, he invariably felt
Like stretching his arms up, as if about to do
A long and lustrous yawn. of course she knew
She had that effect; and whether she lounged or knelt,
Or walked or simply stood, he was never clear
If she was prepared and eager to let him bring
His hands down around her neck, and press her near
—Or would shake her head and permit him no such thing.

This was her talent, to stir both lust and doubt,
She did it the best of all feats she was able;
And therefore other women felt sure she bored
The men she attracted; since all of them, without
Her seeming to provoke them, of one accord
Would yawn and thump their fists down on the table.

ALAN BROWNJOHN

311 *The Latitudes of Home*

HERE I read Biggles; in this chair, *Ulysses*;
Here I watched sperm wriggle across a slide
Slower and slower as their element dried;
In this back corridor I gave secret kisses
To tins of sweet milk, other people's blisses;
Ironed on this table; underneath it tried
To find the pleasure grown-ups used to hide;
And here faced east for several thousand pisses.

Meanwhile my father earned the means of life
At this thin desk; my mother was his wife;
The cost of living rose each dreamy year
Till now: his surgeon, gratis, lifts a knife
And starts to cut him; and I think with fear
Till now I never wrote a poem here.

ALISTAIR ELLIOT

312 *Lachrimae Amantis*

WHAT is there in my heart that you should sue
so fiercely for its love? What kind of care
brings you as though a stranger to my door
through the long night and in the icy dew

seeking the heart that will not harbour you,
that keeps itself religiously secure?
At this dark solstice filled with frost and fire
your passion's ancient wounds must bleed anew.

So many nights the angel of my house
has fed such urgent comfort through a dream,
whispered 'your lord is coming, he is close'

that I have drowsed half-faithful for a time
bathed in pure tones of promise and remorse:
'tomorrow I shall wake to welcome him.'

GEOFFREY HILL

The Worst Fear

313

Some days I do feel better. Then I know
It couldn't come to this, it never would.
I'm much the same as I was long ago
When I could walk two thousand yards, and stand

Upright at parties, chatting. When the men
At petrol stations understood
The words I mouthed. Now is the same as then.
It isn't, though. These are the days when food

Falls from my grip, drink chokes me in my throat
And I'm a nervous nuisance, prone to tears.
The time has come when I put on my coat
With fumbling fingers, grappling with my fears

Of God knows what. Well, I know one that's worse
Than all the rest. My wife's become my nurse.

GEORGE MACBETH

314 *Dreaming*

'OBLIVION, that's all. I never dream' he said—
proud of it, another immunity,
another removal from the standard frame which she
inhabited, dreaming beside him of a dead
woman tucked neatly into a small bed,
a cot or a child's bunk, unexpectedly
victim of some friend or lover. 'Comfort me',
said the dreamer, 'I need to be comforted.'
He did that, not bothering to comprehend,
and she returned to her story: a doctor came
to identify the placid corpse in her dream.
It was obscure; but glancing towards the end
she guessed that killer and lover and doctor were the same;
proving that things are ultimately what they seem.

FLEUR ADCOCK

315 *The Skylight*

You were the one for skylights. I opposed
Cutting into the seasoned tongue-and-groove
Of pitch pine. I liked it low and closed,
Its claustrophobic, nest-up-in-the-roof
Effect. I liked the snuff-dry feeling,
The perfect, trunk-lid fit of the old ceiling.
Under there, it was all hutch and hatch.
The blue slates kept the heat like midnight thatch.

But when the slates came off, extravagant
Sky entered and held surprise wide open.
For days I felt like an inhabitant
Of that house where the man sick of the palsy
Was lowered through the roof, had his sins forgiven,
Was healed, took up his bed and walked away.

SEAMUS HEANEY

316 *Sulpicia*

ROUND this particular date I have drawn a circle
For Mars, dressed myself up for him, dressed to kill:
When I let my hair down I am a sheaf of wheat
And I bring in the harvest without cutting it.

Were he to hover above me like a bird of prey
I would lay my body out, his little country,
Fields smelling of flowers, flowers in the hedgerow—
And then I would put on an overcoat of snow.

I will stumble behind him through the undergrowth
Tracking his white legs, drawing about us both
The hunters' circle: among twisted nets and snares

I will seduce him, tangle his hairs with my hairs
While the stag dashes off on one of its tangents
And boars root safely along our circumference.

MICHAEL LONGLEY

317 *Grandfather*

THEY brought him in on a stretcher from the world,
Wounded but humorous; and he soon recovered.
Boiler-rooms, row upon row of gantries rolled
Away to reveal the landscape of a childhood
Only he can recapture. Even on cold
Mornings he is up at six with a block of wood
Or a box of nails, discreetly up to no good
Or banging round the house like a four-year-old—

Never there when you call. But after dark
You hear his great boots thumping in the hall
And in he comes, as cute as they come. Each night
His shrewd eyes bolt the door and set the clock
Against the future, then his light goes out.
Nothing escapes him; he escapes us all.

DEREK MAHON

318 *The Kaleidoscope*

To climb these stairs again, bearing a tray,
Might be to find you pillowed with your books,
Your inventories listing gowns and frocks
As if preparing for a holiday.
Or, turning from the landing, I might find
My presence watched through your kaleidoscope,
A symmetry of husbands, each redesigned
In lovely forms of foresight, prayer and hope.
I climb these stairs a dozen times a day
And, by that open door, wait, looking in
At where you died. My hands become a tray
Offering me, my flesh, my soul, my skin.
Grief wrongs us so. I stand, and wait, and cry
For the absurd forgiveness, not knowing why.

DOUGLAS DUNN

319 *Ready for Flight*

FROM this I will not swerve nor fall nor falter:
If around your heart the crowds disperse,
And I who at their whim now freeze or swelter
Am allowed to come to a more temperate place.
And if a runner starts to run to me
Dispatched by you, crying that all is trampled
Underfoot, terraces smashed, the entry
Into holy places rudely sampled,

Then I would come at once my love with love
Bringing to wasted areas the sight

Of butterfly and swan and turtle dove
Their wings ruffled like sails ready for flight.

In such surroundings, after the decease
Of devils, you and I would live in peace.

EAVAN BOLAND

320   *On Re-recording Mozart*

WHEN the throb of her voice was cut off, I drove
through streets white with silence: no sound
but my own engine, as if above or beyond
the gear-change a knife glittered, and love

itself were cut out, its high vibrating tongue
docked with a neat flick as the full reel
still turned, clicking, lashing its little tail
at nothing, and silence became her whole song.

Now I have re-recorded Mozart, my tape
unwinding across chasms. Between one note
and the next she still breathes. Her breath

pulls me across darkness, the last escape
of bodies. Rising from her new throat
it redeems and redeems us. I have erased death.

SUSAN WICKS

321 *At the Wrong Door*

A BANK-MANAGER's rapid signature
of hair on the bath enamel, twist
and tail, to confirm that I have missed
you by a minute; mat on the floor,

stamped vigorously with wet; your
absence palpable in the misty,
trickling, inexorcizable ghost
that occupies the whole mirror—

I cannot rub it away—the room
clings to me with such a perfume
of soap and sweat, that I can only

stop to think how somewhere else
you may be standing, naked, lonely,
amid a downfall of dampish towels.

CHRISTOPHER REID

322 *Why Brownlee Left*

WHY Brownlee left, and where he went,
Is a mystery even now.
For if a man should have been content
It was him; two acres of barley,
One of potatoes, four bullocks,
A milker, a slated farmhouse.
He was last seen going out to plough
On a March morning, bright and early.

By noon Brownlee was famous;
They had found all abandoned, with
The last rig unbroken, his pair of black
Horses, like man and wife,
Shifting their weight from foot to
Foot, and gazing into the future.

PAUL MULDOON

323   *The Prince Rupert's Drop*

> *the rapid cooling of this extraordinary glass drop*
> *leaves it in a state of enormous tension . . .*

It's brilliant. It's a tear you can stand a car
on, the hard eye of a chandelier
ready to break down and cry like a baby, a rare
birth, cooled before its time. It's an ear
of glass accidentally sown in the coldest of water,
that sheer drop, rock solid except for the tail
or neck which will snap like sugar, kick like a mortar
under the surefire touch of your fingernail.

It's the pearl in a will-o'-the-wisp, the lantern asleep
in the ice, the light of St Elmo's fire in your eyes.
It's the roulette burst of a necklace, the snap
of bones in an icicle's finger, the snip of your pliers
at the neck of my heart, the fingertip working the spot
which says 'you are here' until you are suddenly not.

JANE DRAYCOTT

324 *Prayer*

SOME days, although we cannot pray, a prayer
utters itself. So, a woman will lift
her head from the sieve of her hands and stare
at the minims sung by a tree, a sudden gift.

Some nights, although we are faithless, the truth
enters our hearts, that small familiar pain;
then a man will stand stock-still, hearing his youth
in the distant Latin chanting of a train.

Pray for us now. Grade I piano scales
console the lodger looking out across
a Midlands town. Then dusk, and someone calls
a child's name as though they named their loss.

Darkness outside. Inside, the radio's prayer—
Rockall. Malin. Dogger. Finisterre.

CAROL ANN DUFFY

325   *Murphy's Law*

A STEP or two inside the door
this looks like all the other London boozers,
strawberry-nosed and ash-haired losers
and just what I'd been looking for:

red plush worn smooth and greasy, mottled,
carpet like a lunch of Jackson Pollock's,
nicotine-yellow ceiling, walls a light shit-brown shading
    to dark,
a choice of draught or bottled
and in the bogs, graffiti from the Ark—
Never mind the Sex Pistols, here's the bollocks . . .

The barmaid tilts a glass with practised hand
and in flows a black swirling sludge. She lets it stand
a minute, I stand transfixed. In flows some more.
You have to let it settle. Get what you settle for.

ALAN JENKINS

326   *A Shortened History in Pictures*

THE Child Maximilian in a White Frock.
The Imperial Family with their Chairs and Pet Cat.
Maximilian, a Thoughtful Young Man in Black.
Maximilian, Emperor of Mexico, at Court.
The Empress of Mexico, his Wife Charlotte.
The Emperor Maximilian on Horseback.
Maximilian and his Court Playing Cricket
(with the English ambassador, Sir Charles Wyke).

The Broken Cacti and the Convent's Outer Wall.
The Execution Squad Standing to Attention.
A Mestizo Leading a Llama under Popocatépetl.
The Execution of Miramón, Mejía and Maximilian.
The Gold-Green Tail-Feathers of the Quetzal.
The Emperor's Shirt after his Execution.

JAMIE MCKENDRICK

327 *In Our Tenth Year*

THIS book, this page, this harebell laid to rest
between these sheets, these leaves, if pressed still bleeds
a watercolour of the way we were.

Those years: the fuss of such and such a day,
that disagreement and its final word,
your inventory of names and dates and times,
my infantries of tall, dark, handsome lies.

A decade on, now we astound ourselves;
still two, still twinned but doubled now with love
and for a single night apart, alone,
how sure we are, each of the other half.

This harebell holds its own. Let's give it now
in air, with light, the chance to fade, to fold.
Here, take it from my hand. Now, let it go.

SIMON ARMITAGE

328 *Sea Sonnet*

THE sea is made of ponds—a cairn of rain.
It has an island flirting up and down
like a blue hat. A boat goes in between.

Is made of rills and springs—each waternode
a tiny subjectivity, the tide
coordinates their ends, the sea is made.

The sea crosses the sea, the sea has hooves;
the powers of rivers and the weir's curves
are moving in the wind-bent acts of waves.

And then the softer waters of the wells
and soakaways—hypostases of holes,
which swallow up and sink for seven miles;

and then the boat arriving on the island
and nothing but the sea-like sea beyond.

ALICE OSWALD

SOURCES AND NOTES

1–3: *Collected Poems of Sir Thomas Wyatt*, ed. Kenneth Muir (1949). **1**: the sonnet may refer to Anne Boleyn. **2**: lever: preferable. **3**: mew: cage. **4–5**: *The Poems of Henry Howard, Earl of Surrey*, ed. Frederick Morgan Padelford (1928). **4**: hap: luck. **5**: chase: chose. Muttrell: Montreuil, where Clere's selfless attention to the wounded Surrey led to his own death. **6**: *Licia*, no. xlviii. *Poems by Giles Fletcher, LL. D.* (1593), ed. Alexander B. Grosart (1876). Minerva: associated with Athena who destroyed her rival Arachne's weaving and turned her into a spider. **7–11**: *Amoretti*, nos. viiii, lvii, lxiv, lxxv, lxxvii. *The Minor Poems*, vol. ii, ed. Charles Grosvenor Osgood and Henry Gibbons Lotspeich (1947). **8**: through-launchèd: pierced through. stours: armed combats. **12**: *Poems of Sir Walter Ralegh*, ed. Agnes Latham (1951). **13**: *Caelica*, no. xxi. *Poems and Dramas of Fulke Greville, First Lord Brooke* (2 vols.), ed. Geoffrey Bullough ([1939]). **14–18**: *Astrophil and Stella*, nos. i, xi, xxxi, xxxix, lxxxi. *The Poems of Sir Philip Sidney*, ed. William A. Ringler, Jr. (1962). **19**: 'The Vanities of Sir Arthur Gorges' Youth', no. lxv. *The Poems of Sir Arthur Gorges*, ed. Helen Estabrook Sandison (1953). embossed: driven to extremity. **20–9**: *The Poems of George Chapman*, ed. Phyllis Brooks Bartlett (1941). i: empery: absolute dominion. iv: lets: hinders. v: species: an emanation (*OED* 5a). cupidinine: lustful. vi: rebateless: undiminished. vii: shows entices: stirs up false appearances. stilled: distilled. ix: forehead: i.e. nib. saise: seize. x: bent affair: directed their efforts. *Lucidius olim*: [it will be] clearer in the future. **30**: *Diana: the praises of his Mistress in certain sweet sonnets* (1592), no. vi. **31**: *Delia and Rosamond Augmented* (1594), no. xlix. **32**: *Idea's Mirror* (1599), no. xi. **33**: *Idea in Sixty Three Sonnets* (1619), no. lxi. **34**: *Du Bartas his Divine Weeks and Works* (1641). The text is unmodernized to allow both the effect of the double acrostic and the choice of reading the sonnets separately or together. The London merchant Robert Nic[h]olson was Sylvester's patron. **36–43**: *Sonnets* (1609), nos. xviii, lv, lx, lxv, lxxiii, xciv, xcvi, cxxxxiv. **44–7**: *Wit's Pilgrimage* (?1605), nos. ix, xxxi, lxix, lxxviii. **48**: Joshua Sylvester, *Du Bartas his Divine Weeks and Works* (1641). **49**: 'Miscellaneous Sonnets', no. xli. *The Sonnets of William Alabaster*, ed. G. M. Story and Helen Gardner (1959). **50**: 'Personal Sonnets', no. xlix. Source as 49. **51**: *Parthenophil and Parthenophe*, no. xliii. *Parthenophil and Parthenophe: A Critical Edition*, ed. Victor A. Doyno (1970). **52**: 'Gulling Sonnets', no. vi. *The Poems of Sir John Davies*, ed. Robert Krueger (1975). **53–7**: 'Holy Sonnets', nos. v, vii, x, xiv, xviii. John Donne, *The Divine Poems*, ed. Helen Gardner (2nd edn., 1978). **58**: 'Certain sonnets', no. ii. *Cynthia. With Certain Sonnets, and the Legend of Cassandra* (1595). **59**: *The Poems English and Latin of Edward, Lord Herbert of Cherbury*, ed. G. C. Moore Smith (1923). Herbert's note: 'Made upon the groves near Merlow Castle.' (i.e. the home of the Duc de Montmorency at Merlou, nr. Clermont). **60–1**: *The Poems of William Drummond of Hawthornden* (1790). **62–5**: *The Poems of Lady Mary Wroth*, ed. Josephine A. Roberts (1983). No. 62 is sung by Philarchos in *The Countess of Montgomery's Urania*. Nos. 63–5 are nos. i–iii of the final section of sonnets in *Pamphilia to Amphilanthus*. **64**: stay: being restrained. **66**: 'Visions', no. vi. *The Poems of William Browne of Tavistock*, ed. Gordon Goodwin (2 vols., 1893). **67–8**: *The Works of George Herbert*, ed. F. E. Hutchinson (1941). **69**: *The Poems of Thomas Carew*, ed. Rhodes Dunlap (1949). **70–1**: *The Poems of William Habington*, ed. Kenneth Allott (1948). **72**: *Poems, &c. Written Upon Several Occasions, And to Several Persons* (1664). **73**: Sonnet iv. William Cowper, *Translations of Milton's Latin and Italian Poems*, ed. William Hayley (1808). **74–9**: Sonnets viii, ix, xii, xviii, xxiii. *Milton's Sonnets*, ed. E. A. J. Honigmann (1966). **74**: conqueror: Alexander the Great. Electra's poet: Euripides. **75**: Lady: Mary Powell. **76**: *Tetrachordon*: the book in which Milton defended his *Doctrines and Disciplines of Divorce*. **77**: massacre of the Vaudois by the Duke of Savoy in April 1655. **79**: Mary Powell or Katherine Woodcock. **80–3**: *Poems on Several Occasions* (1689). **84**: *Lyric Poems*

(1687). **85**: *The Works of Aphra Behn*, ed. Montague Summers (vol. vi, 1915). **86**: Sonnet no. xxvi. *The Canons of Criticism* (1765). Addressed to William Warburton. **87**: *The Poems of Mr. Gray, to which are prefixed Memoirs of his Life and Writings by W. Mason* (1775). **88–9**: *The Poetical Works of the late Thomas Warton*, ed. Richard Mant (2 vols., 1802). **90**: William Hayley, *The Life and Letters of William Cowper* (1803–6). **91**: *Original Sonnets on Various Subjects* (1799). **92–4**: *Elegiac Sonnets* (1784). **95**: *The Poems of Charlotte Smith*, ed. Stuart Curran (1993). **96**: 'Sixteen Sonnets', no. xvi. *The Poems of John Bampfylde*, ed. Roger Lonsdale (1988). **97**: *Poetical Works* (1806). **98**: *Fourteen Sonnets* (1789). No. viii. **99**: *Poetical Works*, ed. Rev. George Gilfillan (1855). **100**: *Poems on Various Subjects* (1823). **101**: *Paul and Virginia* (1795). The sonnet, like the novel, is set in Mauritius. **102**: Sonnet no. xiii. *Sonnets and Miscellaneous Poems by the late Thomas Russell, Fellow of New College* (1789). Nastagio's vision (Decameron, Fifth Day, Tale 8) was of a hunted woman; it enabled him to marry the high-born girl he loved. Ghismonda, daughter of Tancred (*Decameron*, Fourth Day, Tale 1) was given her lover's heart in a cup, added poison and drank it. **103–10**: **105**: his daughter Catherine, died 4 June 1812. **106**: 'The River Duddon', no. xi. *The Poetical Works of William Wordsworth*, ed. E. de Selincourt (4 vols., 1940). **111–15**: *The Poems of Samuel Taylor Coleridge*, ed. E. H. Coleridge (1912). **116–17**: *Psyche, with other poems* (1811). **118**: *The Annual Anthology* (vol. ii, 1800). **119–20**: *Works* (vol. iv, *Poems and Plays*), ed. F. V. Lucas (1912). **120**: Nathan: see Nathan's admonitory parable to David in 2 Samuel 12. **121**: *The Poetical Works of Walter Savage Landor*, ed. Stephen Wheeler (3 vols., 1937). **122**: *Kerhonah, The Vernal Walk, Win Hill, and other poems* (1835). **123–7**: *The Poetical Works of Leigh Hunt*, ed. H. S. Milford (1923). **128**: *The Complete Poetical Works*, ed. Jerome J. McGann (vol. iii, 1981). **129**: *The Christian Year, Lyra Innocentium and other poems* (1914). **130–6**: *The Complete Poetical Works of Percy Bysshe Shelley*, ed. Thomas Hutchinson (1904). **137–9**: *The Later Poems of John Clare (1837–1864)*, ed. Eric Robinson and David Powell (2 vols., 1984). The text regularised. **139**: stoven: tree stem. **140**: *Selected Poems of George Darley*, ed. Anne Ridler (1979). Manuel

Manrique (1795–1823) fought for Venezuelan independence. **141–5**: *The Poems of John Keats*, ed. Miriam Allott (1970). **143**: reply to a sonnet by Reynolds that ended 'Dark eyes are dearer far | Than those that mock the hyacinthine bell.' **146–7**: *The Complete Poetical Works* (1908). **148–50**: *The Complete Poetical Works of Thomas Hood*, ed. Walter Jerrold (1920). **149**: Mme Hengler was firework maker to Vauxhall Gardens. **151**: *Poems of Rural Life in the Dorset Dialect* (1879). **152**: *Works*, ed. H. W. Donner (1935). **153–7**: 'Sonnets from the Portuguese', nos. xiv, xviii, xxi, xliii, xliv. *Poetical Works* (vol. iii, 1873). The title both pretends that the sequence is a translation and refers to her poem 'Catarina to Camoens', where Caterina is a 'Portuguese' dying apart from the poet who had praised her beautiful eyes. **158–9**: *Poetical Works* (1912). **160**: *The Poetical Works of John Greenleaf Whittier*, ed. W. Garrett Horder (1910). **161–5**: *Collected Sonnets old and new* (1880). Nos. cxxxii, cccii, cccvi, cccxvi, cccxxvi. **166**: *Works*, ed. Thomas Ollive Mabbott (vol. 1, 1969). **167–70**: *The Poems of Tennyson*, ed. Christopher Ricks (1969). **168**: to Arthur Hallam. **171**: *A Poet's Harvest Home* (1882). **172–3**: *The Works of Robert Browning* (10 vols., 1912). **174**: *The Book of Ballads*, ed. Bon Gaultier [W. E. Aytoun and Theodore Martin] (1849). **175**: ' "Blank Misgivings of a creature moving about in worlds not realised" ', no. ii. *The Poems and Prose Remains of Arthur Hugh Clough* (1869). **176–7**: *Complete Poems*, ed. N. Scott Momaday (1965). **178–80**: *The Poems of Matthew Arnold*, ed. Kenneth Allott (1965). **180**: The Greeks defeated the Persian fleet off Salamis in 480 BC. **181**: *Ionica* (1858). **182–3**: *The Poems of William Allingham*, ed. John Hewitt (1967). **184**: *England in Time of War* (1856). **185–7**: *Poems of George Meredith*, ed. Phyllis B. Bartlett (2 vols., 1978). **186**: camelus saltat: the camel dances. **188–192**: 'The House of Life', nos. xxiv–xxvii and xlvii. *Poems and Translations 1850–1870* (1913). **193–206**: *The Complete Poems of Christina Rossetti*, ed. R. W. Crump (vol. ii, 1986). ii: text corrected. **207–9**: *Letters between Samuel Butler and Miss E. M. A. Savage 1871–1885* (1935). **210**: *Collected Poems* (1903). **211–13**: *Collected Poetical Works* (vol. i, 1924). **214**: 'Mother and Daughter: an uncompleted Sonnet-Sequence', no. xvi. *Mother and Daughter* (1895). **215**: *Love Sonnets of Proteus* (1881), no. xlviii. **216–19**: *Collected Poems* (4th edn., 1930). **220**: *Poetical Works* (vol. ii, 1874). **221**: 'In the Garden', no. iv. *Poems* (2nd edn., 1877). **222**: *Poetical Works* (1953). **223**: *The Hand in the Dark and other poems* (1913). **224–29**: *The Poems of Gerard Manley Hopkins*, ed. W. H. Gardner (1948). **230**: *Poems, Lyrics and Sonnets* (1882). **231–3**: *A Selection from the Poems of Michael Field* (1923). **234–5**: *Poems of Alice Meynell* (1913). **236**: *Poems of Digby Mackworth Dolben*, ed. Robert Bridges (1911). **237**: *Poems* (1921). **238**: *The Collected Poems of Philip Bourke Marston* (1892). **239**: 'New Poems', no. xcviii. *The Works of Robert Louis Stevenson* (vol. viii, 1922). **240**: *Poems* (1881). **241**: *The Collected Poems, Lyrical and Narrative of A. Mary F. Robinson (Madame Duclaux)* (1902). **242**: *The Works of Francis Thompson* (vol. ii, [1913]). Title: 'Not peace but anticipation'. **243**: *Collected Poems of Mary Coleridge* (1954). **244**: *Selected Poems from The Indian Love Lyrics of Laurence Hope* (1922). **245**: *Land and Sea Tales for Scouts and Guides* (1923). Kipling's note: 'Ithuriel was that Archangel whose spear had the magic property of showing every one exactly and truthfully what he was.' **246**: 'Violet', no. v. *Poems* (1902). **247**: *The Poems, revised*, ed. Richard J. Finneran (1983). **248**: 'Supernatural Songs', no. xii. Text as **247**. **249–51**: *Collected Poems* (1961). **250**: lælaps: Cephalus' dog, which always caught its prey until it met the uncatchable Cadmeian vixen. **252–4**: *Collected Poems, Prose and Plays* (1995). **255**: *Collected Poems* (1978). **256–7**: *Collected Poems 1908–1956* (1961). **258–9**: *The Poetical Works of Rupert Brooke*, ed. Geoffrey Keynes (1946). **260**: *Verses: sixth book* (1938). **261**: *The Collected Poetry of Robinson Jeffers*, ed. Tim Hunt (vol. ii, 1988). **262**: *Collected Poems 1921–1958* (1960). **263–4**: *Selected Poems* (1970). **265**: *By Stubborn Stars* (1938). **266**: *Poems 1924–1933* (1933). **267–8**: *Collected Sonnets* (1941). **269**: 'Fatal Interview', no. vii. Text as **267–8**. **270**: *Complete Poems and fragments*, ed. Jon Stallworthy (vol. i, 1983). Line 9 restores an original MS reading. **271**: Text as **270**. **272**: 'Astro-physics', no. iii. *Collected Poems* (1982). **273**: *The Cicadas and other poems* (1931). **274**: *Complete Poems*, ed. Beryl Graves and Dunstan Ward (vol. i, 1995). **275**: *Marlborough and other poems* (1916). **276**: *Behind the Eyes* (1921). **277**: *Collected Poems* (1949). **278**: *One Hundred Poems* (1944). **279**:

M: One thousand autobiographical sonnets (1938). **280:** *Collected Poems* (1964). **282:** *Come Dance with Kitty Stobling* (1960). **282–3:** *The Winter House and other poems* (1935). **284:** *Poems* (1935). **285:** *Journey to a War* (1939). **286:** 'In Time of War', no. xvi. Text as 285. Nanking: 300,000 Chinese civilians killed there by the Japanese in 1937. **287:** *Another Time* (1940). **288:** 'The Planctus', no. ix (Epigraph), *New Poems 1965–1969* (1969). **289:** *Poems in Praise* (1959). **290:** *Collected Poems of Malcolm Lowry* (1992). **291:** 'The Cancer Hospital' [no. iv]. *Available for Dreams* (1989). **292:** 'Personal Sonnets' [no. i]. *Collected Poems 1930–1955* (1957). **293:** *The Collected Poems of Weldon Kees*, ed. Donald Justice (rev. 1975). **294:** *Collected Poems 1934–1952* (1952). **295:** *The Gavin Ewart Show* (1971). **296:** *Collected Poems 1951–1975* (1975). **297:** *Life Studies* (1959). El: the elevated railway on Third Avenue in New York. Grant: Ulysses S. Grant, Union General elected President in 1868, disgraced by scandal and nepotism, intended as a parallel to General Eisenhower ('Ike'). **298:** *Collected Poems 1943–1987* (1988). **299:** *Earth Walk: New and Selected Poems* (1970). **300:** *Glasgow Sonnets* (1972), no. ii. shilpit: feeble. **301:** *Poems 1943–1956* (1957). **302:** *Collected Poems 1950–1970* (1972). **303:** *The Less Deceived* (1955). **304:** *Selected Poems* (1966). **305:** 'Five Old Favorites', no. ii. *Water Street* (1962). **306:** 'The Price of Stone' [no. xlix]. *New Selected Poems* (1985). **307:** 'The Sanitized Sonnets', no. ii. *The Last of England* (1970). **308:** *The Dust of the World* (1994). **309:** 'Tales of the Islands', chapter ix. *In a Green Night* (1962). **310:** *The Old Flea-Pit* (1987). **311:** *Talking Back* (1982). **312:** 'Lachrimae, or Seven tears figured in seven Passionate Pavans', no. vii. *Tenebrae* (1978). **313:** *The Patient* (1992). **314:** *Selected Poems* (1983). **315:** 'Glanmore Revisited', no. vii. *Seeing Things* (1991). **316:** *Poems 1963–1983* (1985). Sulpicia was a Roman poet, six of whose love elegies survive. **317:** *Selected Poems* (1991). **318:** *Elegies* (1985). **319:** *Collected Poems* (1995). **320:** *The Clever Daughter* (1996). **321:** *Pea Soup* (1982). **322:** *Why Brownlee Left* (1980). **323:** *No Theatre* (1997). **324:** *Mean Time* (1993). **325:** *Harm* (1994). **326:** *The Marble Fly* (1997). **327:** *Kid* (1992). **328:** *The Thing in the Gap-Stone Stile* (1996).

ACKNOWLEDGEMENTS

The editor and publisher gratefully acknowledge permission to reprint the following poems:

Fleur Adcock, 'Dreaming' from *Poems 1960–2000* (Bloodaxe Books, 2000), originally published in *Selected Poems* (OUP, 1983), by permission of Bloodaxe Books.

Simon Armitage, 'In Our Tenth Year' from *Kid* (1992), by permission of the publishers, Faber & Faber Ltd.

Wystan Hugh Auden, 'The Sphinx', copyright © 1939 and renewed 1967 by W. H. Auden and Christopher Isherwood, and 'In Time of War' ('Here war is simple like a monument'), copyright © 1945 by W. H. Auden, both originally published by *Journey to War* (1939); 'Edward Lear', copyright © 1940 and renewed 1968 by W. H. Auden, originally published in *Another Time* (1940); all from *Collected Poems* edited by Edward Mendelson (1976), by permission of the publishers, Faber & Faber Ltd. and Random House, Inc.

George Barker, 'To My Mother' from 'Personal Sonnets' in *Collected Poems 1930–1955* (1957), by permission of the publishers, Faber & Faber Ltd.

Eavan Boland, 'Ready for Flight' from *Collected Poems* (1995), by permission of the publishers, Carcanet Press Ltd., also from *An Origin Like Water: Collected Poems 1967–1987* (1996), copyright © 1996 by Eavan Boland, by permission of the publishers, W. W. Norton & Company, Inc.

Robert Bridges, 'To Francis Jammes' from, *The Poetical Works of Robert Bridges* (OUP, 1936), by permission of Oxford University Press.

Alan Brownjohn, 'Looking at Her' from *The Old Flea Pit* (Hutchinson,

1987), copyright © Alan Brownjohn 1987, by permission of Rosica Colin Ltd. on behalf of the author.

Norman Cameron, 'Fight with a Water-Spirit' and 'The Unfinished Race' from *Collected Poems* edited by Warren Hope and Jonathan Barker (Carcanet, 1990), originally published in *The Winter House and Other Poems* (J. M. Dent, 1935) reprinted by permission of Jane Aiken Hodge.

Charles Causley, 'I am the Great Sun' from *Collected Poems 1951–1997* (Macmillan, 1997), originally published in *Collected Poems* (Macmillan, 1975), by permission of David Higham Associates.

Roy Campbell, 'The Zebras' from *Roy Campbell Collected Works* (Ad Donker Publishers, 1985), copyright © Francisco Campbell Custodio, originally published in *Collected Poems* (The Bodley Head, 1949), by permission of Jonathan Ball Publishers (Pty) Ltd.

John Clare, 'The Ants', 'I am', and 'The Maple Tree' from *The Later Poems of John Clare 1837–1864*, edited by Eric Robinson and David Powell (Oxford University Press, 1984), copyright © Eric Robinson 1984, by permission of Curtis Brown Ltd., London, on behalf of Eric Robinson.

Elizabeth Daryush, 'Children of wealth in your warm nursery' from *Verses: Sixth Book* (1938) in *Collected Poems* (1976), by permission of the publisher, Carcanet Press Ltd.

Donald Davie, 'Jacob's Ladder' from *Collected Poems* (1990), originally published in *Collected Poems* (1972), by permission of the publisher, Carcanet Press Ltd.

Jane Draycott, 'The Prince Rupert's Drop' from *Prince Rupert's Drop* (Carcanet, 1999), originally published in *No Theatre* (Smith/Doorstop 1997), by permission of Carcanet Press Ltd.

Carol Ann Duffy, 'Prayer' from *Mean Time* (1993), by permission of the publisher, Anvil Press Poetry.

Douglas Dunn, 'The Kaleidoscope' from *Elegies* (1985), by permission of the publishers, Faber & Faber Ltd.

Alistair Elliot, 'The Latitudes of Home' from *Talking Back* (1982) in *Collected Poems* (1995), by permission of the publishers, Carcanet Press Ltd.

ACKNOWLEDGEMENTS

William Empson, 'The Ants' from *Poems* (Chatto & Windus, 1935), by permission of Random House Group Ltd. Harcourt, Inc.

Paul Engle, 'Look! The air shudders when you breathe it in' from *Poems in Praise* (Random House, 1959), copyright © 1959 Paul Engle, by permission of Hualing Nieh Engle.

Gavin Ewart, 'The Last Things' from *The Gavin Ewart Show* (Trigram Press, 1971), by permission of Margo Ewart.

Robert Frost, 'Design', 'The Silken Tent', and 'Meeting and Passing' from *The Poetry of Robert Frost* edited by Edward Connery Lathem (Jonathan Cape), copyright 1936, 1942 by Robert Frost, © 1964, 1970 by Lesley Frost Ballantyne, © 1969 by Henry Holt and Co., by permission of the Random House Group Ltd. and Henry Holt and Company, LLC.

Roy Fuller: 'Your Absence' from 'The Cancer Hospital' (no. iv) in *Available for Dreams* (1989), by permission of John Fuller.

Robert Graves, 'The Troll's Nosegay' from *Complete Poems* edited by Beryl Graves and Dunstan Ward, volume 1 (1995), by permission of the publisher, Carcanet Press Ltd.

Seamus Heaney, 'The Skylight' from 'Glanmore Revisited' in *Seeing Things* (1991), by permission of the publishers, Faber & Faber Ltd. and Farrar, Straus & Giroux, Inc.

John Heath-Stubbs, 'Watching Tennis' from *Collected Poems 1943–1987* (Carcanet, 1988), by permission of David Higham Associates.

Geoffrey Hill, 'Lachrimae Amantis' from 'Lachrimae or Seven Tears Figured in Seven Passionate Pavans' from *Collected Poems* (Penguin, 1985), copyright © Geoffrey Hill 1978, 1985, and from *New and Collected Poems 1952–1992*, copyright © 1994 Geoffrey Hill, previously published in *Tenebrae* (1978), by permission of Penguin Books Ltd. and Houghton Mifflin Company. All rights reserved.

Alec Derwent Hope, 'Paradise Saved (another version of the Fall)' from 'The Planctus' no. ix in *New Poems 1965–1969* (1969), by permission of the copyright owner c/o Curtis Brown (Australia).

Aldous Huxley, 'Armour' from *The Cicadas and Other Poems* (Chatto & Windus, 1931), reprinted by permission of the Reece Halsey Agency on behalf of the Aldous Huxley Estate.

Robinson Jeffers, 'Where I?' from *The Collected Poems of Robinson Jeffers*, edited by Tim Hunt, volume 2 (1988). Copyright holder not traced.

Alan Jenkins, 'Murphy's Law' from *Harm* (Chatto & Windus, 1994), by permission of David Higham Associates.

Patrick Kavanagh, 'Inniskeen Road: July Evening' and 'Epic' from *Collected Poems* (McGibbon and Kee, 1964), by permission of the Estate of Patrick Kavanagh through the Jonathan Williams Literary Agency.

Weldon Kees, 'For my Daughter' from *The Collected Poems of Weldon Kees*, edited by Donald Justice (revised edition, 1975), copyright © 1975 the University of Nebraska Press, by permission of the publishers, the University of Nebraska Press.

Rudyard Kipling, 'The Hour of the Angel' from *Land and Sea Tales for Scouts and Guides* (Macmillan, 1923), by permission of A. P. Watt Ltd. on behalf of The National Trust for Places of Historic Interest or Natural Beauty.

Philip Larkin, 'Whatever Happened?' from *The Less Deceived* (1955), by permission of the Marvell Press, London and Australia.

Kenneth Leslie, 'The silver herring throbbed thick in my seine' from *By Stubborn Stars* (1938): copyright holder not traced.

Michael Longley, 'Sulpicia' from *Poems 1963–1983* (Gallery Press, 1985), by permission of the author and Wake Forest University Press.

Robert Lowell, 'Inauguration Day: January 1953' from *Life Studies* (1959), by permission of Farrar, Strauss & Giroux, Inc.

Malcolm Lowry, 'About Ice' from *The Collected Poetry of Malcolm Lowry* (Ediciones Era, 1992), copyright Malcolm Lowry Estate, by permission of Sterling Lord Literistic, Inc. on behalf of the Malcolm Lowry Estate.

George MacBeth, 'The Worst Fear' from *The Patient* (1992), by permission of Sheil Land Associates.

Jamie McKendrick, 'A Shortened History in Pictures' from *Sky Nails: Poems 1979–1997* (Faber, 2000), originally published in *The Marble Fly* (OUP, 1997), by permission of the author and Faber & Faber Ltd.

Archibald MacLeish, 'The End of the World' from *Collected Poems*

1917–1982 (1985), copyright © 1985 the Estate of Archibald MacLeish, originally published in *Poems* (1933), reprinted by permission of the publishers, Houghton Mifflin Company. All rights reserved.

Derek Mahon, 'Grandfather' from *Collected Poems* (The Gallery Press, 1999), originally published in *Selected Poems*, by permission of the author and The Gallery Press.

William Meredith, 'The Illiterate' from *Earth Walk: New and Selected Poems* (Knopf, 1970). Copyright holder not traced.

James Ingram Merrill, 'The Midnight Snack' from 'Five Old Favourites', in *Selected Poems 1946–1985*, copyright © 1992 James Merrill, originally published in *Water Street* (1962) by permission of Alfred A. Knopf, a division of Random House, Inc.

Edna St Vincent Millay, 'Time does not bring relief', 'Grow not too high', and 'Night is my sister' (sonnet vii of 'Fatal Interview') from *Collected Poems* (HarperCollins, 1958), copyright © 1917, 1928, 1931, 1945, 1955, 1958 by Edna St Vincent Millay and Norma Millay Ellis, all originally published in *Collected Sonnets* (Harper & Bros, 1941) by permission of Elizabeth Barnett, Literary Executor. All rights reserved.

Merrill Moore, 'The Odor of a Metal is not Strong' from *M: One Thousand Autobiographical Sonnets* (Harcourt, 1938): copyright holder not traced.

Edwin Morgan, 'A shilpit dog fucks grimly by the close' from *Glasgow Sonnets* (1972), in *Collected Poems* (1990), by permission of the publisher, Carcanet Press Ltd.

Edwin Muir, 'Milton' from *Collected Poems 1921–1958* (1960), copyright ©1960 by Willa Muir, by permission of the publishers, Faber & Faber Ltd. and Oxford University Press, Inc.

Paul Muldoon, 'Why Brownlee Left' from *Why Brownlee Left* (1980), by permission of the publishers, Faber & Faber Ltd. and Wake Forest University Press.

Richard Murphy, 'Beehive Cell' from 'The Prince of Stone' no. xlix, in *Collected Poems* (The Gallery Press, 2000), originally published in *New Selected Poems* (Faber, 1985), by permission of the author, The Gallery Press, and Wake Forest University Press.

343

Alice Oswald, 'Sea Sonnet' from *The Thing in the Gap-Stone Stile* (OUP, 1996), copyright © Alice Oswald 1996 by permission of Oxford University Press.

Peter Porter, 'It's there, somewhere in the Platonic love store', sonnet 2 of 'The Sanitized Sonnets' from *Collected Poems* (1999), originally published in *The Last of England* (OUP, 1970), reprinted by permission of the author.

John Crowe Ransom, 'The Tall Girl' and 'Good Ships' from *Selected Poems* (Carcanet, 1991), originally published in *Selected Poems* (Alfred A. Knopf, 1924), copyright 1924 by Alfred A. Knopf and renewed 1952 by John Crowe Ransom, reprinted by permission of Carcanet Press Ltd. and Alfred A. Knopf, a division of Random House Inc.

Christopher Reid, 'At the Wrong Door' from *Pea Soup* (Faber, 1982), by permission of the author.

Edgell Rickword, 'Moon-talk' from *Behind the Eyes* (Sidgwick & Jackson, 1921). Copyright holder not traced.

Agnes Mary Frances Robinson, 'Art and Life' from *The Collected Poems, Lyrical and Narrative* (T. Fisher Unwin, 1902); copyright holder not traced.

Edwin Arlington Robinson, 'Fleming Helphenstine', 'Lingard and the Stars' and 'Why he was There' from *The Collected Poems of Edwin Arlington Robinson* (Macmillan, New York, 1961), copyright 1935, 1937 Macmillan Publishing Company, copyright © renewed 1963, 1965 Ruth Nivison and Barbara R. Holt, by permission of Simon & Schuster.

Siegfried Sassoon, 'Glory of Women' and 'Sporting Aquaintances' from *Collected Poems 1908–1956* (Faber, 1961), copyright 1918, 1920 E. P. Dutton, copyright 1936, 1946, 1947, 1948 Siegfried Sassoon, by permission of George Sassoon c/o Barbara Levy Literary Agency and Viking Penguin, a division of Penguin Putnam Inc.

Louis Simpson, 'Summer Storm' from *Selected Poems* (OUP, 1966). Copyright holder not traced.

Kenneth Slessor, 'Full Orchestra' from *Selected Poems* (HarperCollins Publishers, Australia), originally published in *One Hundred Poems* (Angus & Robertson, 1944), by permission of the publishers.

Arthur Symons, 'At Seventeen' from 'Violet' in *Poems* (Heinemann, 1919), by permission of Brian Read, Literary Executor.

Dylan Thomas, 'Among those Killed in the Dawn Raid was a Man Aged a Hundred' from *Collected Poems 1934–1952* (J. M. Dent, 1952), by permission of David Higham Associates.

Anthony Thwaite, 'Freedom' from *The Dust of the World* (Sinclair Stevenson, 1994), copyright © Anthony Thwaite 1994, by permission of Curtis Brown Ltd., London, on behalf of the author.

Derek Walcott, 'Le Loupgarou' from 'Tales of the Islands' from *Collected Poems 1948–1984* (1986), copyright © Derek Walcott 1986, by permission of the publishers, Farrar, Straus & Giroux, LLC, also from *In A Green Night* (1962) by permission of the publishers, Faber & Faber Ltd.

Sylvia Townsend Warner, 'To no believable blue I turn my eyes' from 'Astro Physics' no. iii, in *Collected Poems* (Carcanet, 1982), by permission of The Random House Group Ltd. on behalf of the Estate of Sylvia Townsend Warner.

Susan Wicks, 'On Re-recording Mozart' from *The Clever Daughter* (1996), by permission of the publishers, Faber & Faber Ltd.

Richard Wilbur, 'The winter deepening, the hay all in' from *Poems 1934–1956* (1957), by permission of the publishers, Faber & Faber Ltd.

William Butler Yeats, 'Leda and the Swan', copyright 1928 Macmillan Publishing Company, copyright © renewed 1956 Georgie Yeats; and 'Meru' from 'Supernatural Songs', copyright 1934 Macmillan Publishing Company, copyright © renewed 1962 Bertha Georgie Yeats; both from *The Collected Poems of W. B. Yeats*, edited by Richard J. Finneran (1983), revised second edition (1991), by permission of A. P. Watt Ltd. on behalf of Michael B. Yeats, and Scribner, a division of Simon & Schuster.

Every effort has been made to trace and contact copyright holders prior to publication. If notified, the publisher undertakes to rectify any errors or omissions at the earliest opportunity.

INDEX OF TITLES AND FIRST LINES